John Gregory

Song Streams

John Gregory

Song Streams

ISBN/EAN: 9783744775649

Printed in Europe, USA, Canada, Australia, Japan

Cover: Foto ©Thomas Meinert / pixelio.de

More available books at **www.hansebooks.com**

SONG STREAMS

BY

J. GREGORY,

Author of "Idyls of Labour," etc.

Published by the Author.
31, Walpole St., Stapleton Road, Bristol.
1877.

PLYMOUTH:
PRINTED BY G. P. FRIEND AND CO., UNION STREET.

TO MANY KIND HELPERS

OF MY MUSE,

FROM THE OBSCURITY OF LIFE,

I DEDICATE THIS VOLUME,

WITH

PLEASANT MEMORIES,

AND

MUCH LOVE.

J. GREGORY.

PREFACE.

Courteous Reader, by the dim light of a few bottled glowworms I once saw a countryman reading the Bible. This anecdote I pen that you may comprehend the extreme difficulty a toil drudge has to overcome ere he accomplishes the feat of launching into the flood of literature such a volume as this.

Hope not then to find within the compass of my waif-fold the wonders of poesy. Yet here shall you discover flowers you will not disdain, and among the leaves thoughts that shall not be forgotten.

Out on the sea of time I have floated my waifs away as urchins sail paper boats. Here have I again gathered them in; and unto the grace of your indulgence, that they may not with the author soon pass down to greater obscurity, I respectfully commend them.

CONTENTS.

	PAGE.
Summer Clouds	1
Winter Rain	5
Resurrection of Flora	11
Easter Dreams	14
The Storm	19
To Winter	22
In the Garden	24
Leah	26
Jack's Surprise	31
The Northfleet	32
Frolicsome Fan	34
Isolintha	36
Wooing	39
Saint Monday	40
Eve in the City	42
What Art Thou Worth?	44
Gold	45
Decay	46
Questions	49
Dust Thou Art	50
Unsought Pleasure	51
Searching for God	52
The Christmas Box	55
A Memory	58
The May Queen and Her Lovers	59
Eldorado	66
Down Home	68

	PAGE.
THE BELLS	71
THE WHITE SLEEPER	72
THE BROKEN RING	76
SKETCHES OF TWELVE	77
ENGLAND NEUTRAL	81
THE BEAUTIFUL WATCHER	83
RAIN THROUGH THE ROOF	88
THE ORPHANS' CITY, ASHLEY HILL, BRISTOL ...	92
UNDER A CLOUD	95
HYMEN'S ACID	98
THE FUNERAL	100
TO THE WORLD	103
THE OLD PAUPER'S SONG	105
A BOOK	107
SONNETS ON CHATTERTON'S CHURCH, BRISTOL ...	108
HOW MARY DIED	110
RESIGNATION	111
FAME	112
BLIGHTED HOPES	113
A CHRISTMAS IDYL	114
BERTHA	116
SPRING JOYS	137
TO CUPID	139
HAPPY BOB	140
THE MEETING OF THE EMPERORS	141
WHERE IS HEAVEN?	142
WEARY OF LIFE	143
MY GARDEN	145
THE DYING HANGMAN	146
MOTHER TO BABY	147
THE RED MAY	149
GOING TO BED	150

WAIFS.

Summer Clouds.

THROUGH my prison windows gazing
   On the blue midsummer sky,
And the splendour, soul-amazing,
   Of the vapours passing by,
I behold a panorama,
   Motioned by the zephyr's breath,
Passing westwards, 'neath the heavens,
   To the kingdom claimed by death;

Drifting wrecks of Eldorado,
   Bearded bards, with broken lyres;
Temple, palace, and pagoda,
   Turrets, pinnacles, and spires;
Chariots drawn by prancing dragons,
   Mounted knights, and castles grand,
Built on blocks of alabaster,
   Floating o'er my mother-land.

Clouds of every form and tissue,
   Coral tinted caves, from whence

Light-robed phantoms rise and issue
    To the realms of space immense;
Magazines of summer thunder,
    And a host of shapes uncouth,
With the Storm-king's black battalion,
    Marshalled in the misty south.

Headland, peak, and promontory;
    Heaven-piercing hills of snow,
Varnished with a flash of glory,
    Or the sun's seraphic glow;
And the fair earth far beneath it,
    By the heirs of Eden trod,
Lying like a massive emerald,
    Shining in the palm of God.

Fleecy clouds like cherubs' pillows,
    Soft as beauty's silken curl,
Bays of violet with billows,
    Climbing rocks of argent pearl;
And the mighty dead of ages—
    Monarchs, prophets, saints, and seers—
Marching in a vast procession
    To a sepulchre of years.

Symbols of all things uncertain,
    Visions of the empires dead,
Painted on a splendid curtain,
    Fringed with silver, blue, and red:

Pictures sad and pictures pleasant,
   Framed in purple, gold, and dun,
Hung on the blue wall of heaven
   By the palace of the sun.

Winds of summer, while ye wander,
   All the world of glory through,
Tell us what is this new wonder,
   Gliding in my vision new?
It is like a grand cathedral,
   But my fancy seeth more,
She can count the twelve apostles
   Grouped about its lofty door.

Do they listen to a pæan
   From Old England's Sabbath bells,
To the merciful Judean,
   And the tale of love it tells?
Can the bell notes ever wander,
   Wander up and not expire,
Till they reach the heavenly highlands
   Through this sea of summer fire?

There is one day out of seven,
   When a weary child I seem,
Sleeping on the stairs of heaven,
   And it may be all a dream;
But I see the summer angels
   Bearing banners wide and white,

Waving in the summer sunshine
    To the world a sweet good night.

All our lives are drifting tombward,
    While I watch the pageant fair,
" Sheeted shadows" wander homeward
    Through the scented summer air;
And the land is green with beauty,
    But my charm is on the skies,
When the June rose falls to slumber,
    And the Sabbath evening dies.

Faithful hopes of flying treasures,
    Emblems of the hopes we had,
Evanescent as our pleasures,
    Visions, beautiful and glad,
Of the future float above me,
    But my joys are in their shrouds,
While I learn this painful lesson
    From the painted summer clouds.

What is honour, if we gain it,
    But a goblet dashed by fate
From the lips of those that drain it,
    Or a guest that comes too late?
While we wait the banquet endeth,
    While we hope the cloud expands,
While we work some needy brother
    Weaves our shroud with weary hands.

Winter Rain.

AS a bird bereft of feather, or a harp devoid of string,
In this wild, wet, winter weather, I can neither soar nor sing;
I can only sit and listen to the soul-disturbing strain
Of the hissing, seething, leaping, labour-killing winter rain.
It is neither light nor darkness; it is neither day nor night;
It is gloom in all its starkness; it is water in the might.
    Shape and mood
    Of a flood,
   That the winds, a busy brood,
For the love of ruin striving, are all up, and madly driving
   World-ward from the bursting fountains.
    Whence it breaks
    On the peaks
   Of the black and jagged mountains,
    Where the frightened eagle shrieks
    To the blind
    Whirling wind,
   That has not a home to gain,
Nor a grave wherein to moulder
    When it dies.

That is why Boreas tries
To uproot the bedded boulder
From the stony giant's shoulder—
He would hurl it on the valley,
   He would dash it on the plain,
Where the water spirits rally
All their might continually,
     And the rain—
     "Winter rain"—
On the rolling river dances,
Like a sea of silver lances,
To the stormy utterances
   Of the wind that has no pity—
     How it beats
     On the streets
   Of the smoke-enveloped city,
Where the people that you meet
Are a race with "flying feet"
    Seeking shelter,
    Helter skelter,
   From the flood wherein they welter,
To the sad sonorous chorus
Of the turbulent, uproarious,
Winter winds, that wander howling,
To the heavens black and scowling,
Like a herd of lions growling
   In a melancholy strain,
     To the trilling
     Of the chilling,
Labour killing "winter rain."

In my cottage chamber sitting, on its roof I hear
   the rain,
Dash'd from heaven like the splitting of a planet's
   pall in twain,
        By the bluff,
        Burly, gruff,
      Ghostly, gusty, sharp, and rough,
        Forest sacking,
        Ocean racking,
    Winds that wander mercy lacking,
With no home on earth to gain.
        What with me,
        Can the three
    Winds, that are a trinity,
        Want so badly,
        That they madly
Wail about my bolted door
      In the flood descending sadly
From the sea that has no shore?
        How they mob me,
        Rack and rob me;
Will they never more refrain?
      By the soul of my dead mother!
        'Tis no other
Than the winds that drown'd my brother
In the mad Atlantic main.
      'Tis a crowd of things immortal,
Void of body, shape, or form,
'Tis the spirit of the storm;
      Wailing round my bolted portal,

In the rain—
"Winter rain."
What with me can they want hither?
How they murmur and complain!
Till my death-sick fancies shiver
As the thought
Flits before my soul, unsought,
That my brother dead may be
Here with me;
From his grave beneath the free,
Greedy sea,
Where the savage natives wrangle,
For the flesh and blood they mangle,
And the clammy rock-weeds tangle,
Round their white limbs noiselessly.
Is it he?
Hear I not strange footsteps walking
On my haunted chamber floor?
Lord! how loud my fears are talking
In this horrible uproar
Of the rain—
Wind and rain—
That enthrals me in the chain
Of a spell wherein I ponder,
Sick with wonder,
At a tragic scene out yonder,
On the mad Atlantic main,
Where the winds, that shift and bustle
On the flood they lift and ruffle,

With the white-maned monsters scuffle;
    Ah! the prize they hope to gain
      Is a ship,
      That they strip,
    Torture, toss, and overtip,
Till the water-witches clasp her
In a shroud of boiling jasper,
And she disappears for ever, in the reservoir of rain.
Now the widow's eyes are raining
    On the shore,
Now her children are complaining,
    Sorrow sore;
But *the merchant trader, gaining*
    By the loss that made them poor,
    Hears the flighty,
    Wild, and mighty
Winter rain he "wishes further,"
Saying sounds that seem like murder.
    And what more?
Hears a master spirit seeking
    No man's honour, praise or fame,
Hears the noble Plimsoll speaking
    Trumpet-tongued, in mercy's name,
      Pleasure fright'ning,
      Anger brightning   [ning
    Truths, that burn their paths like light-
    To the core
Of the trader's heart, that trembles
As his palsied fear assembles

All his memories terrific, that he fancied dead before
Dares the *traitor* do as Judas did of yore,
    When he dashed a damning token
    Of a greedy spirit broken,
At the feet of bearded rabbis on King David's temple floor,
        With the moan
        And the groan
    Of a soul by God forsaken?
        Oh! the pain
        Of the rain,
And the troubles that awaken
To my spirit, sorrow shaken,
        How it strives
        As it drives
    Comfort from a host of lives.
Now the toiler in the cottage, that hath life and body sold
For a doubtful mess of pottage to the god whose name is gold,
For his famished lovers caring with his rain beclouded eyes,
Through the window looks despairing on the black unbroken skies.
Deeper, wider, passion furious, fetter bursting, freedom fond,
Dashing, with a joy luxurious, down their banks and miles beyond,

Torrents leap,
Bound and sweep,
While the toiler's children weep—
Breadless, wretched, wan, and ghastly,
Famine-pinched and sinking fastly—
Helpless, idle-handed, starving, God have mercy on the poor—
When the winter rain is on them, then the wolf is at the door.

The Resurrection of Flora.

ALL summer-ward flowing,
The spring days are growing:
Aloud March is blowing his trumpet profound,
Because 'tis his duty
To waken up beauty,
And summon the dead from their graves in the ground.

Swift sunbeams are streaming,
On primroses beaming,
Where wood-doves sit dreaming in wind-shelter'd dells,
And bird music gushes
From fresh-budding bushes
To violets smiling in moss-matted cells.

The ice-king is dying,
The frost fiends are flying
From spring, hither hieing o'er mountain and plain;
See! where they have striven
A snow robe lies riven,
The spear of the crocus hath pierc'd it in twain.

Away from Death's keeping
Fair things that were sleeping
Come timidly peeping—awoke by the blast
Of March, the spring angel,
In summer's evangel,
Proclaiming to Flora that winter is past.

Where all things seemed blighted,
Dear daisies are sighted,
And lambs leap delighted to see them spring up;
No king in his palace
Lifts such a fair chalice
As my fairy goblet, the bright buttercup.

The dead are ascending,
From sepulchres rending—
Their death night is ending, their rising is grand;
Their freedom is spoken,
Their bondage is broken,
The spirit of life is abroad in the land.

Behold them assembling,
All tenderly trembling—

That future resembling, of which we have fear,
    When life shall be given
    To spirits sin-shriven,
And they shall be lifted to heaven's high sphere.

    I love for their daring,
    Beyond all comparing,
My March flowers bearing a message of love:
    From them we can borrow
    This solace in sorrow—
Like them we may blossom all trouble above.

    Through darkness uptoiling,
    All troubles outfoiling,
No neighbour despoiling to be what they are;
    They blow on our mountains,
    They glow by our fountains,
And sparkle like gems on the brow of a star.

    All summer-ward flowing,
    While spring days are growing,
And March is here blowing his trumpet profound;
    With them we are going
    From all we are doing—
Like them may we rise from our beds in the ground.

Easter Dreams.

WHEN to the playground of the lamb,
 Over the lea from dainty cells,
The belted, bronzy, brown bees swam
 To kiss the golden cowslip bells,
  And more than this,
In the delightful Easter hours
When Psyche from her prison foul,
  In search of bliss,
Sprang out to life a wingèd soul,
I nestled on a bank of flowers,
  Breathing the breath
   Of blossoms bright,
  That were from death
   To life and light.
Woke by the children of the sun,
  Which ye call beams,
Who do the Poets' banquet shun,
Or fail to feast your souls on dreams,
And from my bed of green and gold
Beneath the boughs, above the mould,
I saw in the blue wold aloft
A fleecy, fair, fantastic, soft
Slow-sailing swarm of silver white
Summery clouds, that in my sight
Swam as a vessel on the deep
Swims when the saucy sea winds sleep,

And Fancy of the clouds above,
Sang thus to please my happy love.

After the days of mighty March,
   The burly trumpeter of Spring,
Are numbered 'neath the world's blue arch,
   When orchard trees are blossoming.
It is a joy the Father grants
Unto the blest inhabitants
Of that high home all else above,
Where all the people live on love,
That they may quit their blissful spheres,
       To live and smile
       A happy while
On this wild wilderness of tears,
Which is the star God loveth most,
Of all the great harmonious host.
And a death-haunted orb from whence
   Christ, for the love of Adam's race,
Arose to the magnificence
   Of endless life, from Death's embrace.

Therefore the pilgrim angels leave
That bliss, for which we fret and grieve,
       In happy crowds
       And fleecy clouds,
Sailing above this world so far,
Are unto them as ships afloat
In the blue sea about a star,
Or each of them a pleasure boat,

Wherein the pilgrim angels glide
From heaven in the Easter-tide.
      Hark! o'er the land
      A joyful band
Of minstrel birds on blissful wings,
      Ascend to meet
      The angel fleet;
All the green wood with music rings;
      And spirits sweet,
        From blossoms fair
      Arise to greet,
        On wings of air,
Them to this world that we call ours:
Hence they are wafted by the breath
Of wonders from the house of death
      Called April flow'rs;
For all these pilgrim ships that glide
      Along the blue
Bright heaven in the Easter-tide
      Are made of dew—
The dainty dew of herbs and flowers,
Which, in the holy Easter-hours
Fell on them in the starlight mild,
As tears upon a sleeping child
Fall from the milder orbs of love,
Bending its virgin babe above.
And there are clouds of which we know
They were not from the seas below,
Nor from the rolling river's breast
Raised to such peaceful states of rest.

There is among
That snowy throng
Of sunny clouds that swim and shine
Up in the bright
Blue sea of light,
A floating fount of love divine,
Made of that passion-tide which swept
From mercy's heart when Jesus wept;
And when the pilgrim angels glide
From heaven in the Easter-tide;
'Tis from that fount, the world above,
They drink his tears, and say, " What love!"

Thus to the muse that I love best
Fair fancy sang at love's request,
And even as I heard her sing
Her happy theme—
Was it a dream?
I saw the heavens opening;
Not with the sound of sudden haste,
But as a languid lily's mouth
Opens at noon to catch the chaste
Kiss of an air wave from the south;
So softly opening more and more,
Up in the skies,
Until mine eyes
Seem'd looking in through heaven's door,
And through that door an angel throng,
With tender sounds of holy song,

Came; and before the angels flew
Down to our planet's beach of blue,
A flock of doves, and by that beach,
Within the pilgrim angels' reach,
  So light afloat
   A cloud of dew,
  Shaped as a boat,
   Swam in my view.
And then—and then, that fairer boat,
Than ever fancy found afloat,
Drawn by a flock of doves along,
Came sailing with the angel throng;
Nearer, and nearer yet, until,
High on a heaven-piercing hill,
  Out in the west,
  I saw it rest,
And from its bounds the happy band
Leapt light as snow flakes on the land.
Then from the earth beneath their feet
Brake a bright host of blossoms sweet,
Such as were never brought by spring,
Save to a soul's imagining;
So I believe that they were brought
From heaven by the happy thought,
For mine were as that blissful throng
Of doves that drew the boat along;
And if thine inner eyes are good,
When that thy mind is in the mood,

And if on such a bank of flowers,
You nestle in the Easter hours,
More than I saw you may behold,
And sweeter may your dreams be told;
Mine is a little earth child's lay
With whom 'twill pass away.

The Storm.

THE winds are up, the clouds are down
    About the mountain's waist,
The sky is black as murder's frown,
    And wild as anger's haste.
Death rides the blast that flings the spray
    High as a forest tree
Over the doom'd ship in the bay,
    And tumult shakes the sea.

Hark! how the gusty monsters roar,
    The stoutest vessel's form
Shakes as a reed on Albion's shore
    In this tremendous storm.
God or Britannia? which is now
    Chief Ruler of the waves?
To whom do the tall breakers bow
    Above our sailors' graves?

Come down to the rock-belted beach,
    And the wild ocean's rim;
There you shall hear the sea-gull screech,
    To see the lifeboat swim:
Lord! how she leaps from wave to wave
    Toward the sinking bark;
It is a chariot of the brave,
    And the sea lions' ark.

See, how they bend the ashen blades
    To climb the seething wall;
Now bulwark deep she bravely wades
    The flood at duty's call.
She cleaves the breaker's crest in twain,
    And, like a thing of life,
She revels in the stormy main,
    And glories in the strife.

What pale spectator of the fight
    In this wild midnight noon
Is this, that trembles with affright?
    'Tis the fair Lady Moon.
The pall of clouds is rent to rags,
    And shatter'd fragments fly
Before the blast like hunted stags,
    Or aught that fears to die.

God speed the lifeboat to and fro,
    And hear us while we plead—

It is a fearful task we know
    To dare the noble deed.
Oh, which will win, the wind or flood?
    There will be calm—but then,
This is the fear that chills our blood—
    The stakes are living men.

Weird voices haunt the troubled air—
    Hush! there it is again;
I wish mad Fancy would not swear,
    'Tis like the soul of Cain
Wailing for shelter from the fiends
    That mob it by my door;
I pray that it may be the winds—
    The winds, and nothing more.

Just where the robin loves to sing,
    Atop my chimney gray,
There is some horrid howling thing
    That will not go away.
A violent hand my window shakes,
    I wonder why 'tis so;
There may be peace when morn awakes—
    But what a night for woe!

Brides of the bold that plough the deep
    For glory, love, or hire,
With you we will this vigil keep,
    Till all your hopes expire.

The storm that blew your joy away
   Our pity woke to life;
'Tis hard to keep despair at bay—
   God help the sailor's wife.

She wanders in her chamber's girth,
   The sport of horror foul;
Love tells her of a brave man's worth,
   Fear whispers to her soul:
The blast that shakes your cottage door
   Blew from his graveyard wide:
Woman, you will not see him more—
   God help that sailor's bride.

She bends, she kneels, she tries to pray,
   But 'tis so wild and dark;
Distracted love may lose its way,
   And prayer might miss its mark.
Her fancies are a raven flock,
   Her faith a wounded dove,
Down by the beach, on a bare rock—
   God bless that woman's love.

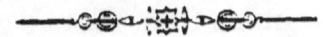

To Winter.

AVAUNT! Away, thou gloomy ghoul,
   Exalt thy shadows from my soul;

And from the sky its grimy shroud,
Or give me strength to burst this cloud
Of dense depression, foul, and vast,
Wherein my wings are tangled fast,
So that I cannot soar to sing;
Avaunt, that I may welcome spring.

Up! and shake off thy dusky guise,
Awake the airs which clear the skies,
That I may see the winter stars;
This is the time when gallant Mars
And belted Saturn dance above
Our world with Venus, Queen of Love,
And silv'ry beams of glory flow
From fair Diana's graceful bow.

Come in thy better raiment clad,
Bring rosy health to make us glad,
Let the dry sands of Afric drain
Deep, as it loves, thy gushing rain,
From fountain clouds that never tire.
Then will I hail thee, glorious sire
Of gentle Spring, thy Master gave
To roll the stone from Flora's grave.

It is not day, it is not night,
When shall I see the angel Light
In the blue heavens, lifting high
His splendid torch? Avaunt! and die,

Or speed thy change, for with thy gloom
Thus, thou hast made this world a tomb,
Wherein some sickly sunbeams stray
To tell us when it should be day.

In the Garden.

IT is the hour we used to meet
    When thou wast in thy prime,
So we for love will make a fete,
    In mem'ry of the time—
In mem'ry of the time we met,
    When first I came to woo, Nan;
And just that we may not forget,
    I'll tell thee what to do, Nan.

The king of day out in the west,
    Wrapt in his golden gown,
Sinks on his crimson couch to rest,
    So drop your knitting down;
And let us in the garden spread
    Our supper on the mould, Nan,
Then will we dream of bliss ahead,
    Just as we did of old, Nan.

Down where the tall sunflow'rs flare
    Their blossoms to the bees,

There we will turn our backs on care,
    And give the hours to ease;
My arm about thy waist shall creep,
    Just as it did of yore, Nan,
When all the wealth I longed to keep
    Lay clasped within its store, Nan.

There! it was just like this we sat,
    Down in our wooing days;
And then you gave my cheeks a pat,
    Because I sang your praise;
And then I saw your blushes flower
    In all their pretty prime, Nan,
Ah! that was young Love's sowing hour,
    But now's the harvest time, Nan.

Bring out the Holy Book, good dame,
    Ere doth the day expire,
And read a chapter by the flame
    Of God the Father's fire;
And then let all the children sing
    Their evening hymn aloud, Nan;
There may be angels listening,
    By yonder shining cloud, Nan.

Look at our bouncing bairns, my lass,
    Are they not joys of ours,
Skipping about the garden grass,
    Breathing the breath of flowers?

Now give them each a kiss for me,
  Unto the little last, Nan;
And I will do the same to thee,
  In mem'ry of the past, Nan;
    The past, Nan—
    Thou wast, Nan,
A wit more fond of Love's salute
  When wooing in the past, Nan.

Leah.

SHE walks the earth with such a grace,
  As grief alone can wear;
And when I meet her face to face,
  'Tis more than love can bear
To see the seal of sorrow set
  On all that once was fair.

The glee is gone from her blue eye,
  And from her life the light;
Where the sea-wind wails wander by,
  She starteth with affright,
As if she heard a sad man's voice,
  Saying, "My love, good-night!"

And this was how it came to be;
  (I know her sorrow well)

There was a cot from trouble free,
    Down in a sea-land dell,
Where loving Leah's laughter rang,
    Blithe as a bridal bell.

I loved her with a brother's love,
    I loved her as a man,
My love was as a mother's love,
    So pure for her it ran;
And that is why I mourn to see
    That wreck of beauty wan.

There came a warrior of the wave
    My love and hers between,
He was so gallant, good, and brave,
    And wore a noble mien;
'Tis more than half a sin to say
    I wish it had not been.

She gave her life to John the Bold,
    And well she keeps her vow;
His love was worth a mint of gold;
    Where doth he linger now?
The curlew cries his grave above,
    And mournful breakers bow.

I wish sad Leah would not stray
    Down where the sea weeds grow,
Watching strange vessels in the bay,
    That wander to and fro;

Sure John the Bold would never stay,
   If death would let him go!

Down to the beach, one stormy night,
   She hastened from her bed;
Her cheeks were of a ghostly white,
   Her lips were like the dead,
And burning tears fell from her eyes,
   As drops of molten lead.

The winter winds like demons glad
   Did rave, and bark, and yell;
Crash on the coast the breakers mad
   In dreadful fury fell;
The stars were in a pall of cloud,
   Black as the roof of hell.

Along the beach the life-boat men,
   Smitten with terror sore,
Beheld a woman's shape; and then,
   Above the tempest roar,
Three times they heard her shriek aloud
   "John Hore! John Hore! John Hore!

You said that you would come to me,
   And yet thou art not here;
I lift my hands in vain to thee,
   I cry; thou dost not hear;
Come home, come home, come home; O God!
   My soul is sick with fear.

Hence from my bed, at Love's command,
    I came the watch to keep;
If thou art in death's icy band,
    Why should I live to weep?
O God! and I am on the land,
    But thou art in the deep."

That thought was as an arrow shot,
    Deep in her troubled breast:
They led her to her sea-land cot;
    They laid her down to rest:
Never a cottage in the land
    Contains a sadder guest.

She plies her needle with a sigh,
    And then she tries to sing;
But when her mem'ries wander by
    It is a painful thing
To see the pent-up torrent gush
    From misery's bitter spring.

Memories that wake at Love's commands,
    To walk with muffled feet;
They carry tablets in their hands;
    They wear a winding sheet;
And chant the praises of the past,
    When life was nectar sweet.

I often say within my heart,
    How sweet her grief must be!

She will not spare one little part
    Of her full cup to me;
I wish she would not bar me from
    Her soul's Gethsemane.

Grief is a flower that loves the shade
    Where joy can never grow;
And there's a night by sorrow made,
    That may no morning know;
But night is when the spirit stars
    Put on their golden glow.

So shines her love-star clear and strong,
    Although my grief may say
" Alas; 'twill not be shining long
    Within its shrine of clay;
Hush, when the sun burns through the cloud
    I know it will be day."

Bright through the snow the crocus breaks,
    The primrose from its urn
Wakes with a smile; but to her cheeks
    The rose will not return;
'Twas John the Bold that stole the rose,
    Poor Leah lives to mourn.

Jack's Surprise.

OVER the silver sea afar,
    Over the silver sea,
What joy hast thou brought for me, Jack Tar?
    What joy hast thou brought for me?
'Tis nearly a year you sailed away,
Over the bar and out of the bay;
There's never an hour of every day,
    But what I have prayed for thee.

What would you have me bring you, Poll?
    What would you have me bring?
A silken gown? a monkey droll?
    Or a golden bird to sing?
What was it I promised of all things fine—
Parrots? or pearls? or rings to shine?
What was it I promised if you'd be mine,
    From over the sea to bring?

" You promised that if I kept my vow
    A gift you'd bring to me?"
"Come hither, my lass, and take it now;
    'Tis here in my mouth," quoth he.
"There; that same kiss I carried away,
Over the bar and out of the bay;
I give it back to thee to-day
    Sweet as you gave it me?"

The Northfleet.

SO near the shore that she no more may gain,
    Our pilgrim ship at anchor in the night
Lay trusting to her deep sea cable's strain,
    Full manned and ready for her ocean flight.

And as a flock of wild sea swans at rest,
    Swam wingèd rovers of the distant seas
Around her on the liquid monster's breast,
    With pinions folded to the adverse breeze.

"The watch was set," and bright each beacon lamp,
    Tinging the robe of night with mellow sheen,
In the black wold above our ocean camp
    Shone as a fun'ral torch in hands unseen.

Hushed were the voices of the pilgrim host,
    In the great gloomy hold clasped by the sea,
That hurled its breakers on the Kentish coast
    With a strange, wild, sleep-scaring monody.

Swift as the snow-clouds sailing o'er the skies,
    And bearing down to where the Northfleet lay,
A demon of the flood with gleaming eyes
    Came on her course o'er the wind-troubled bay,

Straight as the dart of death; on through the gloom
    Dashed the sea-demon on our pilgrim ship,
That trembled, shook, and hasted to her doom,
    Crashed as an egg-shell in a giant's grip.

In leapt the green waves through her shattered frame,
  Drinking the pilgrims' lives, but the foul foe
Stole from the death scene, and a deed of shame
  To friendly darkness, reckless of our woe.

Braves to the pumps, and heroes to the leak,
  Sprang for the love of life, and fought the flood
The feeble shrank from, with a thrilling shriek
  For help and mercy, in their wildest mood;

Till the sad captain gave his weeping wife
  To the bold boatswain on his shoreward route;
Then from our helpless exodus of life,
  And every heart, the Angel Hope went out.

Yet every chance of life was madly sought
  By the convulsive clutchings of despair;
There was a rush of frenzied crowds that fought
  For boats entangled in the doomed ship's gear.

There were strong men that mute as statue stones
  Of milk-white marble crouched on their own tomb;
There was confusion, and heart bursting groans,
  Farewell embraces, and vain thoughts of home.

And skyward darting, signals of distress
  In quick succession from the sinking ship
Shot o'er the troubled bay of Dungeness,
  Sharp as a death-scream from a mortal's lip.

D

Oh! wandering pilot, answering to the sign,
  That o'er the billows drove thy conquering steed,
I wish, good master, that the joy was mine
  Of thy life-saving in the dreadful need.

Brave was the skipper, and his noble crew
  Obedient to the end, well winning praise
Out of the horror that around them grew,
  In the sad ending of their dang'rous days.

But brave in vain, when the great climbing wave
  Over the bulwarks came on board too fast,
Folding three hundred victims in one grave,
  And wrangling for sad clusters on the mast.

Then the great coffin, with its living load,
  Plunged as a diver to its ocean bed;
The Northfleet lies at anchor on the road,
  Britannia mourns for her three hundred dead.

Frolicksome Fan.

"WHITHER away,
    Fanny, my fay,
Bright as a beam of this sunny spring day?"
Spake a fond mother, and frolicksome Fan,
Under the blossoming apple-trees ran,

Singing " Sweet mother, I speed for a run
Over the meadow-land under the sun."

    Down by the stile
    Whist'ling the while,
Who is it waits for a merry maid's smile?
Fanny and I when the daisies were out,
Went with the butterflies dancing about—
Dancing about in the merry May hours,
Over the meadow-land covered with flowers.

    In a green nook,
    By a bright brook,
Where the fringe blossoms delighted to look
Out from their bowers of delicate green;
On their fair images shrined in its sheen;
Together we chatted, and love was our theme,
Over the meadow-land down by the stream.

    Nobody knew
    How my love grew,
While the lark sang to us up in the blue,
Beautiful, summery, heavens above,
Ringing with music and glowing with love,
Down in the days when our wooing begun,
Over the meadow-land under the sun.

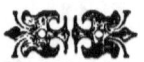

Isolintha.

The subject of this poem was drowned in the Bristol Channel.

IF you will not ask me more
   Till the well of grief is dry,
And my weeping days are o'er,
   I will truly tell you why
'Tis I wander all in vain,
With my monologue of pain,
By the deep, sad heaving sea.
It is always grieving me,
For beneath its billowed breast,
Lies my first love, last, and best,
      Isolintha!

Through the fountains of the sun,
   In a garden and a grave,
Where the bearded sea vines run,
   And the wild sea flowers wave;
Where the blue sea spiders crawl
Up the trellised coral wall,
Lies a sleeper, wan and lone;
On a bier of ocean stone,
Lies the form that loved me most,
And the best of beauty's host,
      Isolintha!

By a phosphor spirit's torch,
   Scaly shapes, with gleaming eyes,

Sailing in her chamber porch,
    Search the cell she beautifies.
And these people of the sea,
Crowding round her curiously,
Lift her tresses as they float
To the monotonous note
Of the surge that beats a beach
You will never rise to reach,
        Isolintha!

Led by love, my fancy dives
    Through the palpitating sea
To a tomb wherein she strives,
    Yes, she strives to welcome me;
Strives to draw her matted hand
From its glove of golden sand,
But the danky sea-weeds twist
Clammy bracelets on each wrist;
And that sheath of yellow sand
Is the grave of beauty's wand,
        Isolintha!

To thy prison-house afar,
    Was it love that lit me down,
Or that briny, blood-red star,[*]
    Gloaming on thy temple crown?
Awake! my Isolintha, dear!
O, my soul, she does not hear.

        * The star fish.

Do I dream, or am I dead,
In this hideous, deep sea bed?
If my soul was not thy slave,
Should I love thee in this grave,
    Isolintha?

I have wept sad years to death,
    Since the wild, heart-rending wave
Drank my darling's parting breath,
    And the prayer her white lips gave.
Not a zephyr seaward goes,
With the sweets of Devon's rose,
But it bears a tremulous strain
From the gusty song of pain.
It is years, long years ago,
Since I learnt to love thee so,
    Isolintha!

If my love was not so blind,
    Should I foster vain regret
For the casket left behind?
    When the gem is heaven-set,
Where the jewels of mercy bloom,
Shall we seek it in the tomb?
As a sea bird on the deep
Folds its wings and falls to sleep,
Thy sweet spirit floats above,
On a flood of better love,
    Isolintha!

Musing by the sea, I saw
    Through my tear-beclouded eyes,
Heaven's love in nature's law,
    And a path to Paradise :
Saw a path by spirits trod,
From the crucible of God.
When the sun was drawing rain
From the fountain of the main,
Rose a spirit from its thrall,
Whom her sister angels call,
    "Isolintha!"

Wooing.

"DORA dear, Dora dear, come, and sit down with me;
Under the boughs of this shadowing hawthorn tree,
Hid in this mossy nook, who can discover us?
'Tis like a summer cloud, shining all over us,
    Here may I tell thee my love without fear,
    Come, and sit down by me; Dora, my dear.

Dora dear, Dora dear, be not so shy of me,
'Tis not a kiss I am wanting to buy of thee,
Talk not a word about little birds listening;
For by the light of thy merrie eyes glistening,
    They shall confess to me all that you mean,
    Come, and sit down by me, Dora, my queen.

Shook by the breath of the wind-spirits, whispering,
It is of love that the light leaves are lispering,
It is for love the wood pigeons are cooing so,
Down in the dingle, and I must be wooing you,
    Wooing you, darling, my fate to decide,
    Come, and sit down by me, Dora, my pride.

Dora dear, Dora dear, when shall our wedding be?
Say to my heart, 'neath this sweet odour-shedding tree,
Whisper me tenderly; tell me my dutiful;
When shall our village bells warble most beautiful
    Stories of love in the valley below?
    Name me the day I am longing to know."

Spake the fair Dora; "'Tis much that you flatter me,
Sure, 'tis your tongue is a gun in love's battery;
So my affections must certainly fall to you,
And my objections are nothing at all to you:"
    Colin kissed Dora, and under the tree
    Settled the day when the wedding should be.

Saint Monday.

Come on, Saint Monday; thou art not the most
    Unwelcome ghost
Of a dead yesterday that ever came,
    In robes of flame,

From a day's sepulchre in the far west,
To rouse the toiler from his Sabbath rest.

Much may I wonder why men call thee Saint,
      Yet there's a quaint
Dash of indulgence in thine aspect odd,
      As if the rod
Of care was broken by some angel's hand,
When Sabbath bells were warbling o'er the land.

Morn o'er the city breaks, the stars are few
      In the great blue
Wide wilderness above, and fading fast
      Out to the past,
The pilgrim day is passing through the dawn;
Street lights expire, and sleepy watchmen yawn.

Sharp chanticleer to the departing stars,
      Up through the bars
Of the dim cellar looks, and trumpets loud
      To the fair crowd,
With a brief preface made by flapping wings,
Cries, "Allelujah! praise the King of kings."

Hark! through the city ways from slumber's camp,
      How the loud tramp
Of Labour's legions, led by duty stern,
      Sounds the return
From Mercy's banquet to a new week's strife,
For home, love, beauty, fortune, fame, and life!

For at the bidding of his master man,
      Loud as he can,
The Giant Steam doth as a demon shriek,
      And myriads break
From the soft bonds of sleep, with a strong will,
To battle Want; they have no hope to kill.

The drowsy sluggard, like some Samson shorn,
      Turns from the morn
His sheeted face, and for the loss of time
      Cares not a dime;
He will at breakfast say to sulking wife,
"I did not hear the whooter 'pon my life."

But come, Saint Monday, for I do not dread
      My cross of lead;
'Tis not the load we bear nor the road's length,
      But the soul's strength
Which proves the hero, and if toil's a ban
Then 'tis the best that ever fell on man.

Eve in the City.

NOW to the toiler comes a sweet reprieve;
    The curfew bell of labour o'er the gate
Of the great factory swings, and hope elate,
We throng with weary hands because 'tis eve,
    Out on our homeward paths, and silence steals
    In the deserted wilderness of wheels:

And busy hands in humble homes prepare
    All that they can for the bread-winners' sake;
    The kettle-steam is up; new bloaters bake;
Afresh the floor is swept, and father's chair,
    In its accustomed place, with cushioned seat,
    Waits for a traveller in the thick thronged street.

Nor may it wait in vain, some from their toil,
    Like weary soldiers when the fight doth cease,
    Will with their mates to smoke the pipe of peace,
To the near tavern hie, though suppers spoil,
    And watching wives are cross when husbands say
    " 'Twas but one pint to help me on my way."

Now, with their torches kindled at the fount,
    The swift lamp-lighters run; the shadows fly
    To the dim courts and lanes; and as a sky,
Swarming with stars 'twere past all hope to count,
    So glows the city, with the light that shines
    From the fire spirits in their crystal shrines.

The streets are noisy with a host of sounds;
    His Evening *Echo* the news-vendor rings;
    Fiddles are squeaking to a wight that sings;
Clarionets chatter, and the harpist wounds
    Music to death amid the mingling cries,   [pies!"
    Of "Fine new walnuts!" "Oysters!" and "Hot

It is the hour of love in every sphere,
    And love is not a stranger to the poor;
    Mary the servant, at her master's door,
To hear a pleasant voice say "Well, my dear,"

Waits in her apron white with cheeks aflame,
Because she hopes to change her place and name.

And from her mirror in the sphere above,
   Emblazoned beauty turns; a splendid thing,
   Reared in the lap of fashion, she will sing
In the saloon below her dreams of love,
   Or on the sofa lounge, then to the play,
   Ride with her lover in a graceful way.

The weary children to their beds are put,
   And some of them will cry their souls afar
   Unto the land of dreams where fairies are
Playing bo-peep, and till their eyes are shut,
   Others will lie and sing their vesper psalms,
   Happy as cherubs 'neath the heavenly palms.

What Art Thou Worth?

WHAT art thou worth, lord of the castle proud,
        Out of thy shroud,
To those that fear thy law, look, frown, or word,
        As 'twere the sword
Of Fate suspended by one hollow hair,
Above the thread of life, sharp, bright, and bare?

What art thou worth? Shut up thy door and count
        The full amount

Of all thou hast to love and leave behind
         When thou'rt a blind,
Poor, senseless, nothing, mingled with the earth.
What art thou now? What wilt thou then be worth?

And thou, O king, that should'st all men surpass;
         What to the mass
Of wealth-creators art thou worth of good,
         More than the brood
Who fawn, cringe, kneel, and lick thy royal hand
For a luxurious living in the land?

The sun bears light, the clouds bear rain, the sod
         Bears like a god
For man, brute, bird, and insect, every need;
         But man bears greed
That knows no limit; Oh! my mother earth,
What unto love are thy best children worth?

Gold.

MY heaven is not paved with gold;
    For all that hath been writ of it,
I would not have it if I could,
    There's blood on every bit of it.

I would not harm my angel's feet
    With such a hateful use of it;

I loath, I scorn the thought unsweet,
    Because of man's abuse of it.

Love weeps insulted by the thought;
    Shame on the saints that sing of it;
The world is cursed because 'tis sought,
    And demons love the ring of it;

Love it, because that souls unwise
    Polluted with the stain of it,
That might without to Eden rise,
    Run hell-ward for the gain of it.

Worms of the world, how mad you are!
    What glory can you see in it?
Why bear your gold god up so far?
    How strong your faith must be in it!

Tear the idea from your creed;
    Let not your fancies dwell with it;
My thoughts that dare a better deed
    Would pave the streets of hell with it.

Decay.

WHEN shrivelled leaves are dropping dead
    From rocking trees; and home to bed
  The sleepy roses haste away;
There is a spirit in the land,
It is my grief to understand;
      It is Decay.

It was to hear the robins' psalm
I wandered where the zephyr calm
   Did sob, and moan, and seem to pray,
And there I saw what you may see—
A spirit making signs to me;
      It was Decay.

On mossy wall with ivy clad
Sweet robin sang, but I was sad;
   And yet it was a tender lay,
Such as I love the best of all;
But then I heard a spirit call;
      It was Decay.

Calling me from the fight for bread
With man my foe, and home to bed,
   As one that loved me from my play,
Did often in the evening hours;
Ah! she is with the sleeping flowers,
      Gone to Decay.

Gone, in the way I have to go;
Why should my spirit answer "No?"
   Am I not weary of the fray?
If that my lamp of faith be bright,
Enough to last me through the night,
      Why fear Decay?

Why fear? O thou weird spirit speak,
Hast thou not from my lady's cheek

Stolen the last red rose away?
Till there is not a bud to cull
　　Of all that once was beautiful:
　　　　　Tell me, Decay?

Dear brow, from which these gray hairs fall,
Alas! it is the fun'ral pall
　　Of all my love implores to stay
With me because 'tis mine; and when
We part it will be death.　What then?
　　　　　Answer Decay!

Avant! thou foul relentless hag!
My wild love weeps to see thee drag
　　This idol of my soul away
To thy dark den and clammy couch;
See! how it shrinks at thy vile touch.
　　　　　Avaunt! Decay!

Art thou a friend ordained to lead
The weary to the rest they need?
　　After thy night will it be day?
Then gently, gently, lead us both
Along the road, though love be loth.
　　　　　Welcome, Decay!

Questions.

Do the flowers know
   Pathways of escape
From the house of death below
The evanescent snow,
  Unto beauty, life, and shape?
Have they hope or faith to show
How a mighty hand unseen
Leads them up the blades between?

Does a birdie beg
   Knowledge how to break
From its native egg,
   When its yellow beak,
To a world unseen before,
   Opes a little crisp white door,
And a happy mother chuckles to the sweet
Pretty baby chick that crieth wheet?

   Knowledge more than these,
     Why should we desire?
   For what God doth please,
   With thy soul at ease,
     Wait; and to life aspire:
So shall thy aspirations be
Thy wings to immortality.

Dust Thou Art.

THE weather was dry;
    The roads were brown;
Out of the sky
    The wind came down;
And under the elms that shook with dread
    Over my path,
    Along the strath,
My mother I met, when mother was dead.

    My mother! how odd!
        Was she not put
    To sleep by God?
        The door was shut
Of her chamber strange, and we made her bed
        Under a mound
        Of holy ground;
Yet mother I met, when mother was dead!

    My mother unsought
        I often meet,
    With a weird thought,
        Out in the street,
Coming along in a shroud that trails
        Over the red
        Perishing dead
Leaves that follow with windy wails.

Thy mother is just
    The same as mine;
My mother is dust,
    And so is thine,
Whether a king, or beggar instead:
    And so, alas!
    It came to pass
My mother I met, when mother was dead.

Unsought Pleasure.

WHERE the sorrows of the city most abound,
    I was walking with a chilly autumn day,
Saying, "Here is not a pleasure to be found;"
    So I gave my thoughts to misery away—

Gave my sorrows to the people of the street—
    Gave my pity to their poverty and pain,
Till I found a pretty pleasure at my feet,
    In a little shining shallow pool of rain.

'Twas a picture of the heavens up above;
    Do you say it was a very common thing?
I have laid it in the treasury of love;
    I am looking at its beauty while I sing.

For while bending o'er the shallow water-pond,
  I cared not for my sorrow in the street,
I was lifted all unhappiness beyond,
  By the thought of heaven being at my feet.

Searching for God!

WHAT is there in this world like Thee;
  Thou, great Eternal! One in Three?
And Three in One Almighty 'kind,'
Imperial God! must I be blind
Till death reveals the secret? which
Of all Thy wonders vast and rich,
Beyond conception shall I ask
To aid me in this ponderous task?
Say loving Sun, whose happy beams
  Dance on the dazzling snow,
And light us through this world of dreams
  With thy seraphic glow;
Canst thou to me this knowledge give?
Art thou like Him by whom we live?
Is it that power of might immense
Which holds the planets in suspense,
And will to waste no atom spare?
Is it, O Lord, of love and care;

That arch of beauty angel built,
Above this flowery realm of guilt,
The summer rainbow? Can it be
That liquid monster named the sea,
Which folds ten thousand wonders in
Its awful compass? May we win
The secret from Thy winds? 'tis odd
And strange of sound that thought within
    Should say
There is no power so much like God
As that to which the pine plumes nod
On the tall mountain's brow; there may,
There must be truth in this, the air
 Through which the happy sunbeam darts
Unseen, but present everywhere,
 Is made of three distinctive parts
Essential to one whole: the wind
Ah! there's the key I longed to find!

What man, or brute, or creeping thing,
Blades, bees, or trees, or birds that sing,
In the Creator's empire grand
Could dare its certain death withstand?
Shorn of this mighty vast unseen
And God-like wonder, what between
This star from which my fancy runs
To the blue sea of golden suns
Is there that can arrest and strike
The soul with truth like this? 'tis like

Him in its omnipresence more
Than all my thought beheld before;
It is the all-sustaining breath
Of life; without it would be death,
And if it be a likeness poor,
Still am I richer than before.
Now then my soul thou shalt not fear
The sceptic's laugh, or scornful sneer,
For when they press me in the fight,
And when they grow with boastive might,
I will to save me from despair,
Invoke three spirits of the air:
Carbo shall to my aid descend,
Hydro shall be my second friend,
Bright Oxygen, the third and best,
Shall haste to conquest with the rest,
And Truth declare that there can be,
Three all in One, and One in Three.

The Christmas Box.

HOW much shall I give for that smile you are
      sporting?
Come; what shall I give you, my little lady;
I know very well you are only come courting,
    You cherry-cheeked rogue climbing up on my knee;
        With happy hopes feeding
        Some joy of thy needing,
And eyes that are pleading most eloquently.

Come; what will you take for the ring of your
      laughter?
A bow for your hair? or a tart for your tea?
I ween 'tis a kiss you are toiling up after,
    So on, and be welcome to one, two, or three:
        'Twas ever the duty
        Of manhood to beauty,
Thus then I salute thee, my little lady.

What! not want a kiss? well, the next time I offer,
    You may not refuse me, you shy little fox;
Pray tell me your pleasure, my beautiful scoffer,
    With white fingers tangled about in my locks?
        Now why do you tarry,
        My ruby-lipped Carrie?
"I want you to give me a nice Christmas box."

Ah! just like the world; I am waiting, and willing;
    But what shall it be? I am longing to know;

Suppose that you change me this new silver shilling
    For one kiss of yours; 'neath the mistletoe bough,
        Where Cupid, for pleasure,
        Lurks shooting at leisure,
His victims that measure love ribbon below.

Well done, my wee lady! that settles the matter;
    And now I will tell you a story beside;
But first you must promise to hush your love chatter,
    Although 'tis a pity your tongue should be tied
        Except you were trying;
        The power of crying,
Instead of just sighing for fancies denied.

About in the kingdom of trouble and danger,
    Abroad in the desert through which I have been,
Where grief is the native, and joy is the stranger,
    What strange Christmas boxes there are to be seen
        In places death-blighted,
        Where life lies benighted,
And love weeps affrighted, to see what I mean.

Such quaint fashioned boxes, prepared for enshrining
    Fair soul-worshipped jew'ls when their beauty is fled,
Provided with pillows, and warm flannel lining,
    So that you might fancy 'tis just like a bed
        Prepared for a lover,
        And then you discover
A name on the cover of somebody dead.

You knew Dolly Downing, the love poet's daughter,
  Dear Dolly; of whom that we all understood,
How tender-armed angels to heaven up caught her,
  Away in the spring of her life's golden-hood,
    From caring, from fretting,
    And all the begetting
Of evils besetting the pathway to good.

Well, 'twas on a time when the laurel and holly
  Were gracing our homes as you see them to-day,
That one of these boxes for dear little Polly
  Was brought to her chamber, and in it she lay
    Cold, waxen, and chilly,
    And dreadfully stilly,
Just like a dead lily gone down to decay.

Ah! now thou art weeping, my dear little lady,
  Because I have led thee the shadows among;
Thy world was all sunshine, but now 'tis so shady,
  And I have been doing thee, doing thee wrong;
    Alas; 'tis thy pity,
    And more than my pity,
That sorrow should enter thy heart with my song.

A Memory.

I WILL sing to thee, O lady of my lay!
   I will sing to thee sweet memories of mine;
I will charm thee with a story of a day,
   When thou wert the merry maiden Madoline.

By the margin of a river in the west,
   We sat beneath a canopy of oak;
I made thy cheek a pillow on my breast,
   And the boughs came down about us like a cloak.

'Twas a sunny summer Sunday, Madoline,
   And the honey winds that wandered up the dells
Came upon us o'er the wavy water shine
   Of the river with a melody of bells.

And we listened to their music as we sat,
   Till a butterfly, soft yellow as a moon,
Came and hovered o'er the roses in your hat,
   On that sunny summer Sunday afternoon.

You may mind it, gentle lady, if you try;
   You may see a pleasant picture of my love,
In the fluttering of that yellow butterfly—
   Your pretty summer coronal above.

I saw that thou wert beautiful and good;
   I knew that humble poverty was mine;
I forsook thee in thy merry maidenhood;
   I have saved thee from its sorrows, Madoline.

The May Queen and Her Lovers.

A Legend of St. Vincent's Rocks.

UP St. Vincent's lofty shoulder,
    Mounted on a massive boulder,
In what time the grace of Flora decks the flowery
    woods of Leigh,
    You *may* see the spectre dreary
    Of an old man, sorrow weary,
Crying "Mary, Mary, Mary," in the midnight,
    crying "Mary!
    I am coming home to thee."

    Then the shadow riseth slowly,
    From its resting place unholy,
And with silent feet it wanders by the mountain's
    flowery rim;
    But the raven in its eyrie
    Hears a pilgrim solitary
Passing by its sanctuary, crying for the soul of Mary
    In the summer starlight dim.

    Tombless, as the winds of heaven,
    Homeless, poor, and unforgiven,   [span;
Solemnly it wanders onward to the Avon's splendid
    Then the spirits of the river
    Tremble with a sudden shiver,
And they murmur "Lost for ever," as the shining
    waters sever
    To receive the hopeless man.

'Tis a secret worth your finding,
And a lesson worth our minding,
What the expiator meaneth by his melancholy cry,
In the haunts he loved of olden,
When the world was green and golden,
Ere his future was unfolden, ah! this truth has been withholden,
'Tis the way he went to die.

In the chronicles of sorrow
I have read the tale we borrow,
And a little, tear-stained story, written with the tell-tale pen
Of a man, whose spirit weary,
Glideth by the raven's eyrie,
In the midnight lone and dreary, crying "Mary, Mary, Mary!"
By St. Vincent's hawthorn glen.

'Twas that time in merry England
When the butterflies went Maying
Through a scented sea of sunshine,
To the carol of the skylark,
To the jingle of the blue bells,
To the whistle of the mavis,
To the brown bees' psalm of labour,
And the cooing of the wood dove,
Sitting like a summer angel,
On a canopy of emeralds.

Then I saw a band of damsels,
Saw a flock of joyful beauties,
With my merry May Queen Mary,
Tripping on the soft green heather,
In and out among the daisies,
And my heart grew full of praises,
And my soul, with tender trouble,
Full of trouble, fond and "tender,"
As a river's mossy cradle
Where the virgin waters bubble,
Full of passion, loved and loving;
As a blossom-bannered orchard
In the gentle reign of April,
When the baby buds are peeping
From their cloisters in the fruit trees.

Fondly from the dance I won her—
Won my darling May Queen, Mary—
When her fairy feet grew weary,
And we rambled from the dancers
O'er the glorious downs of Clifton,
On the flower-bespangled carpet,
To a temple of the Graces
In the groves of love and beauty,
Near the violet-broidered border
Of Saint Vincent's lofty kingdom.

Then we nestled down together,
And I told my love to Mary—

To my trembling, trusting Mary;
And my little, loving May Queen,
Till she fed my love with kisses,
Purer than the pearly dewdrops,
Shining out from golden goblets
In the heart of Flora's palace
And our sacred mountain altar.

In what time our guardian angels
Wandered up through heaven's gateway,
Laden with the blessed record
Of our blissful spirit bridal,
Up toward our Eldorado
Came my mad love rival, stalking;
As the lithe fur-footed tiger,
As the demon of the jungle,
Came my mad love rival creeping
Up toward our sinless Eden.

In and out among the hawthorns,
Wheeling upward from the valley,
As a falcon to a dove's nest,
Came my wild half-brother, Walter.
And his cruel eyes were blazing
With a fearful lust for murder,
As he halted by a boulder,
By a tilted, bedless boulder,
Listening to a fiend that whispered
"Take revenge and hurl it on them;

Fool, or coward, hurl it on them!"
Then the mass came crushing on us,
Right across our narrow pathway,
And it smote my golden idol—
Smote my gentle, trusting Mary,
And my little, loving May Queen,
Lifeless—in the vale below me.

When I felt my life was blasted
With this horror everlasting,
Up the cliff I sprang toward him,
Gifted with a strength Satanic;
But he fled before my vengeance
As a stag before the hunter.

In the cavern of the giants—
In the Giants' Cave I found him—
Found the murderer of Mary.
Face to face I met and fought him,
There we wrestled in the darkness,
And we fought the fight of devils,
For my madness never left me,
And his fury knew no dying,
Till I wiped my bloody fingers
On the sweat-damp hair of Walter;
Then I left him to corruption.

Floating down the flossy Avon
Came a full-winged outward bounder,

And she bore me far from England
O'er a realm of tumbling waters
With one terrible companion,
For my mem'ry never left me.
Up and down the earth I wandered,
Sowing tears and reaping anguish.
I have taunted Death to take me
In the fields of England's battles,
I have tried to drown my sorrow
In a thousand lakes of vine blood.
I can bear my woe no longer,
I will rise and go to Mary—
To my little, loving May Queen.
She will pray to the great Spirit,
" To the Queen of all the angels,"
She will say " Have mercy on him."
What? She comes! she comes! toward me;
Oh, how kindly, kindly, kindly.
See! she beckons! 'tis no vision
Fading from me. Mary! Mary!
Oh, my little, loving May Queen!
Thee I follow! thee I follow!
What is this between us lying?
'Tis the cloven skull of Walter,
And my feet are tangled, tangled,
Tangled in the hangman's halter!
Oh, this horror! never dying.
I am as a sea-fish prisoned
In a lake of poisoned water,

And my heart's a haunted ruin.
So it was, it was a vision;
Yes, my heart's a haunted ruin,
Where the only thing I cherish
Is a hate of life that blossoms
When I hear the laugh of children.

After forty years of penance
I am here in hated England,
Sitting where I sat of olden,
When my world was green and golden.
'Twas not love that led me hither,
But my pitiless tormentor;
She is faithful as my shadow
In this haunted grove of hawthorns,
Where the butterflies are Maying.

She is with me; there! before me—
Crouching on the silken heather,
Playing with poor Walter's tresses;
Pointing to my bloody fingers;
I will wash them in the midnight,
In the Avon's flossy water;
I will cast my withered body,
I will fling my spirit's fortune,
Through the ambient air of heaven,
From the Avon's span of iron.

Here the story that we borrow
From the chronicles of sorrow,

Cometh to its sad conclusion, and this is the reason why,
> You *may* see the spectre dreary
> Of an old man sorrow weary,

Walking by the raven's eyrie, crying, "Mary, Mary, Mary!"
> 'Tis the way he went to die.

Eldorado.

'TWAS on the brow of Brandon Hill,
   My lassie and her lad O!
Sat side by side, as lovers will,
   Beneath the hawthorn shadow,
Dreaming dreams of a world that beams
   By the name of Eldorado.

Shyly his arm about her waist
   Crept in the hawthorn shadow;
Four red lips met one joy to taste,
   And softly to her lad O!
Quoth the maid, "How far from the world where we are
   Is the world called Eldorado?"

"Near, pretty near," sang a bird to the lass;
   "Near, pretty dear," said the lad O!

"In a place named Morrow, to which we pass
　　Away from the hawthorn shadow;
By the honeymoon's light we shall sail in sight
　　Of the realm called Eldorado."

He made her vows on the velvety slope,
　　And she made vows for the lad O!
He planted a flower in her heart, called Hope,
　　And blithe from the hawthorn shadow
They went through a church together, in search
　　Of the land named Eldorado.

Little maids came with the lassie's grace,
　　And boys grew up like the lad O!
But the rose lieth dead on a mother's face,
　　And care is there, like a shadow
Of evil to meet in a life made sweet
　　By the search for Eldorado.

Very merry years are down with the dead,
　　Grief is come to the lad O!
The hair hangs grey from a matron's head—
　　They are near to their Eldorado;
'Tis a bed underground, called Rosemary mound,
　　In the "Valley of Death's dark shadow."

Down Home.

OH, the day is gone to rest,
    And I revel in the beams
Of a moon in yellow drest,
    That hath brought me happy dreams
Of a love-enchanting spot,
And a little moonlit cot,
        Down home.

And fair spirits of my race
    Crowd about me, as I lie
Dreaming of that happy place,
    With the yellow moon on high,
Beaming, as it loved to beam,
On the joys of which I dream,
        Down home.

Soft as butterflies that sit
    On the blossoms they love best,
So my winged fancies lit
    By the moon in yellow drest,
Nestle down upon my heart
Till my memories depart
        Down home.

And I dream with open eyes
    Pleasant dreams I must adore,
Of that pretty paradise,
    With a being at the door,

Calling, in a gentle way,
To a little lad at play,
        Come home.

In the molten mellow light
  Of the yellow moon above,
She is looking very white;
  But her voice is full of love,
Full of love, that seems to be
Like an angel's call to me,
        Down home.

Home again, at love's desire,
  Merry, innocent, and glad,
Romping by my father's fire
  With a kitten frolic mad,
And a bonnie brother boy,
Laughing like the soul of joy,
        Down home.

Swinging on my garden swing,
  As I swung in days of yore,
When the trees were blossoming,
  Forty years ago or more.
Thanks to mem'ry, strong and kind,
For that swing I left behind,
        Down home.

Sailing with the sweetest lass
  Heaven ever made for love,

On a liquid looking-glass
   Of the summer stars above.
Singing, as we used to sing,
When the hills were echoing,
      Down home.

With her, from my care afar,
   Walking in the witching light
Of a primrose-coloured star
   That hath lit my dreams to-night;
Happy, beautiful, and good,
In our glorious goldenhood,
      Down home.

Leaning o'er the bridge at eve,
   Listening to the charm that wells
O'er a scene I wept to leave,
   From a band of dancing bells;
Silvery bells that sang to me
Up a sacred orchestra,
      Down home.

Ah! the spell is breaking fast,
   But the bells are tinkling still,
Faintly in that happy past,
   And my spirit in their thrill
Trembles out, in blissful tears,
For the dear departed years,
      Down home.

There's a coffin cloud above,
   With a silver-broidered pall,
And the yellow moon I love
   Lies within its massy thrall;
So the joys whereof I sing
Are all visions vanishing,
           Down home.

The Bells.

MERRILY, cheerily, hark! how sweet
   Old England's bells are pealing!
     Whilst the swift globe,
     In her green robe,
Among the stars is wheeling;
     And as we race
     The realms of space,
They blend love-peals of laughter,
     As if they fain
     Would banish pain
To death for ever after.
Come, gentle zephyr, whisper low,
And tell me, for I long to know,
Where do the sweet bell spirits go
     That wander from our tower?

Peacefully, pleasantly, hark! those bells
Proclaiming love's evangel!
  Flow dulcet stream
  Of notes that seem
Sung by my soul's good angel.
  Blow, gentle breeze,
  Bearing heart's ease,
For spirits upward climbing
  To heaven's rest,
  Are cheered and blest,
When Sabbath bells are chiming.
Many a soul, long steeped in crime,
Bends softened by their holy chime,
For mem'ries of a better time,
  Float from the old church tower.

The White Sleeper.

I STOOD in the night
 Bending over the bed
Of a sleeper so white
 That I fancied her dead;
For lilies that sleep
 On the water-nymph's breast,
When honey winds creep
 Out of groves in the West,

To fan the faint flowers
　　Up from a sweet swoon,
Nor birds in their bowers,
　　Beneath the May moon,
Ever slept such a sleep as my love in her bed—
That I leant above saying, "Alas, she is dead."
　　Not the golden-eyed stars,
　　　　Nor their yellow-robed queen,
　　Peeping in 'twixt the bars
　　　　Of our crystal-like screen,
　　Ever halted their cars
　　　　To behold such a scene,
　　Except when they sight
　　　　Radamanthus, that steers
　　His course in the night
　　　　From the fountains of tears,
　　That gush to betoken
　　　　Love's saddest farewell,
　　When Psyche has broken
　　　　The bonds of her cell:
　　'Tis then that they brighten
　　　　Their torches of gold,
　　Lest darkness should frighten
　　　　Shorn lambs of the fold,
　　That tremble and tighten
　　　　On Jesus their hold,
　　When flying from trouble
　　　　Unto that blest shore
　　Where pure pleasures double
　　　　And pain is no more.

These were the sweet words
   Of a song by desire,
Hope sang to the chords
   Of her peace-making lyre;
And so love delighting
   Kept singing, till fear
My spirit affrighting,
   Spake thus of my dear:

"The lark from its flight
   O'er the green meadow's breast,
Cometh down with delight
   To its daisy-fringed nest;
But her soul shall not come
   From the land of its dreams
To this rose without bloom,
   And this star without beams,
Where pleasure is greatest,
   And purest and best,
Where love is the sweetest
   That ever was blest;
Her sweet soul is ranging
   Away from thine own,
With bliss ever changing,
   By mercy bestown;
And thus while it tarries
   With angels above,
Thy mother earth carries
   The corse of thy love.

Look! man, void of valour,
    Look down on that bed!
The fair sleeper's pallor
    Is that of the dead!
Her cheeks shall not redden,
    Her eyes never shine;
Those white hands, so leaden,
    Shall never clasp thine,
Nor own thy caresses:
    Haste, man, while you may,
Snatch one of her tresses
    From Death, and away;
So few are the blisses
    Humanity sips,
Thy warm passion kisses
    Lie dead on her lips.
Come! come! from that altar
    Spill not the sweet wine,
Let true Love exalt her
    In Memory's shrine."
Thus Fear, the inventor of horror, too wild,
Became my tormentor, but Hope, Heaven's child,
That watched the pearl wicket, detected a breath
Coming through the pearl thicket to say 'twas not
    death;
Soft eyelids are lifted, sweet pinky lips part,
And sorrow is drifted away from my heart.

The Broken Ring.

Too loud thy lips have spoken
   Prophetic words of woe;
Our bridal ring is broken,
   And we are breaking too:
This is our parting token,
   Alas! what shall we do?

Come back, false Hope, that flattered
   My loving soul to sing,
Before our darlings chattered
   The songs of life's young spring;
And thou swift Time that shattered
   This dear old bridal ring.

Give me this hand, sweet weeper,
   You gave me with your vow,
When love made thee my keeper,
   And beauty crowned thy brow;
Thus with affection deeper
   Than then, I clasp it now.

Oh! pilgrim day departing,
   Can thy successor bring
Balm for my spirit smarting,
   Or chase the fears that sting
My frightened thoughts upstarting
   O'er this time-shattered ring?

Sketches of Twelve.

WHEN Janus leaps
Up from the bed
Of his poor dead
Mother, that sleeps
Out in eternity; and the winds freeze
Waters to ice,
Is it not nice
Over the river to travel at ease,
Swift as a sprite, by the skeleton trees?

When his days ebb
Out to the past,
And in at last
Snowy-faced Feb.
Comes, is it not very pleasant to sit,
Warm as a mouse,
Home in your house,
Near as you please, where the fire lies lit,
Working, or reading, or learning to knit?

When it is March,
Tossing brown dust
From the earth's crust,
To the world's arch,
Over the tree tops, and sunbeams are strong,
Is it not fun
To see the run

Of the white snow from the hills with a song,
Down to the valley lands laughing along?

    When April sweet
      Comes with her showers,
      And happy flowers
    Under your feet
Break from the house of death, and the birds sing,
      Who can be sad?
      You should be glad,
As the brown bees that are out on the wing,
Over the meads where the cowslip bells ring.

    When it is May
      Is it not good,
      Out in the wood,
    From cities away,
With some one you love to sit down on the stump
      Of an old tree,
      Looking to see,
And guessing how far the red squirrels can jump,
Over the beech trees that grow in a clump?

    When o'er the globe
      June to our isle
      Comes with a smile,
    In a green robe
Spangled with roses—white, yellow, and red—
      And by the wall
      Ripe cherries fall

Down in her lap by the strawberry bed,
Is not this world like a heaven you tread?

    And when July
        Sunbeams are shot
        Fiercely and hot
    From the blue sky,
So that fair flowers fall faint on the lea,
        And of the pond
        Cattle grow fond,
As you are fond of a shadowing tree,
Is it not beautiful down by the sea?

    When with her scythe,
        Over our earth,
        Mocking dumb dearth,
    August the blythe,
Laughs like a god! with delight doing good,
        And there are sweet
        Cakes of new wheat,
Made for the hearty brown harvester's food—
Is it not merciful? is it not good?

    But when for sport
        September's in,
        Is it not sin
    Of a sad sort
To be out with your dog and your murderous gun,
        And, without shame,
        Sneaking for game,

Along by the hedges where partridges run ;
The deed is ignoble, and better to shun.

October appears—
Leaves to decay,
Hasten away ;
Clouds are in tears
For the dead that lie thick in the lanes, and we seem
Breathing the breath
Of them in death,
While musing amid them ; till fondly we dream
Of a spring that should gladden our souls with its
beam.

November gloom
Falls from above ;
Now let me love
My little room ;
If I look out to the skies overhead,
I see a stark,
Dirty, half dark,
Vapour-full wilderness, and I must tread
Mud in the streets, with umbrella aspread.

Brief the days die,
Long is the night,
Making its flight,
Under the sky,
When with December the year is of age,

To be no more,
Now as of yore,
Holly-crowned Christmas and Pleasure his page,
Happy as ever are crossing the stage.

England, Neutral.

LET England watch her water gates
   By headland, cape, and bay;
    While rivals fight
    For wrong, or right,
Let her sons watch and pray.
    Back from the brawl;
    Ah! one and all,
Peace is our guest to-day;
But watch ye well her water doors,
   Prepare for come what may.

Oh, skipper! standing at the helm
   Of freedom's barque, what cheer?
    The war blast howls,
    The tempest growls,
The storm will be severe;
    God keep thy heart
    By honour's chart,

And teach thee how to steer,
With gentle force,
A noble course
From the dire danger near!

I mind a hymn I sang of yore,
And thus it used to go—
"Let dogs delight
To bark and bite,
For God hath made them so."
It is to me
A mystery,
That God the deed should do;
Are kings to sway,
Made in that way?
Is it their nature, too?

Kings fight; I wrong them, they are grown
Wise in these latter days;
Our modern kings
Are sacred things,
More than they were always.
The hours have been
When kings were seen
Armed; at their armies' heads,
Leading the charge
Like fiends at large;
But, now, they die in beds.

So let them die, till wars are boons,
With all my throbbing heart
I pray; and sing,
God save that king
Who plays a kingly part!
But he who plans
That worst of bans,
War, with its blasting strife,
Doth quit his throne
To turn the stone,
While Murder grinds her knife.

The Beautiful Watcher.*

A TRUE STORY.

"WEAVE me a song, my father,"
    Spake my darling with a sigh,
And I saw the tear-clouds gather
    Like dew in a violet's eye;

* My son being a schoolmate of the Hero's brother, came home laden with a little lock of the Beautiful Watcher's hair, and entreated that I should (to use his own language) make some verses in memory of the tragical occurrence. The heroism of Archibald Walters must be the admiration of all. The whole calendar of immortals on the muster roll of Fame does not present another such. Why are the Lords of song silent? I have listened in vain, and regret that I have not paid sweeter tribute to the noble Spirit.

    The tragic event related in these lines occurred on October the 23rd, 1874.

Like dew pearls shrined in the tender
   Girth of a violet's cup,
     Trembled a tear,
     In the eyes of my dear,
When the sigh of his soul came up.

"Of what shall I sing, my beauty?
   Come, give me a theme to weave,
To please thee is surely my duty,
   With what do you come to grieve?"
I looked in the face of my darling,
   And watched for the sound of his breath,
     As a maid for a kiss,
     But alas! it was this;
"It is all about death, 'about death.'"

His cheek on my shoulder reposes,
   I start at his earnest request,
As bees from the bosoms of roses,
   Sad sighs wander up from his breast.
I knew they were stealing the sweetness
   Of life from the soul of my child,
     And leaving their sting,
     In a blossom of spring,
But I said, as I mournfully smiled,

"What, love, wilt thou pay me for singing,
   If I should obey thy command?
And what art thou tenderly bringing
   To me in thy lily white hand?"

"I bring thee O father, a treasure,
  I want to be kept like a vow,
    It is one golden lock,
    From a death-smitten flock,
And a curl from brave Archibald's brow."

I look in the face of my glory,
  I gather my strength for the strife,
And bid him relate the grand story
  Of heroic Archibald's life.
The tears from his eyes trembled over,
  His cheeks are all snowy and wan,
    His loving lips part
    With a sob from his heart,
And thus to my heart he began.

Saying, This is the way it was, father,
  That he came to be turned into clay,
It was nearly the last of October,
  Because 'twas the twenty-third day.
When he said to his mother, "Come, kiss me,"
  And just like a chick from a coop,
Sped away for the fun to be caught in a run
  On the road at the back of a hoop.
Away from the city he wandered,
  As if 'twere appointed by fate,
And a strange little boy that he met in his joy
  Came with him to be his playmate.

I wish you would mind to remember,
  His age was but six when he gave
His life up so free to the lad only three,
  That he perished in trying to save.

Away they went further and further,
  Till the little strange boy said, "I know
If we just go up here, there's a place pretty near,
  Where such bouncing big blackberries grow."
So in the lone lane, without thinking,
  What sorrow might follow their joy,
For the love of the sweet bramble berries,
  He went with the strange little boy.
Until all at once, when the darkness
  Fell down on the world like a blind
From the beautiful windows of heaven,
  Their homes were a trouble to find.
All round by the tall tangled hedges,
  They went, till 'twas growing quite late,
And the shadows came crowding about them,
  To keep them away from the gate—

Came down from the clouds of October,
  Around them like curtains of crape;
And they listened with hearts beating wildly,
  To voices of things without shape.
For when the weird shadows were wafted
  About by the winds to and fro,

They went with a moan, and they came with a moan;
  So I wish you would tell if you know,
Was it, father, the wicked field fairies
  That wanted their lives to destroy?
For I feel sore afraid, he was surely waylaid
  By them, with that little strange boy.

Oh! 'twas such a night to be out in,
  So bitter, so long, and so bleak,
With no home to be found, and no bed but the
    ground,
  And the strange little boy was so weak,
That he said, "I can't walk any longer,"
  And then he crouched down on the clod,
With his burden of pain, weeping tears like the rain,
  For the want of his mother, to God.
But he went off to slumber while weeping,
  And beautiful Archy above
Stood keeping the watch, like an angel,
  Because 'twas for nothing but love.
For it was not for gold he kept watching,
  It was not for fame to be won,
Nor was it for praise that he ended his days,
  In the heroic way it was done.

Ah! what was it then, my wee darling,
  What means did brave Archy employ
When the night winds came howling and snarling,
  Around the poor little strange boy?

He took off the clothes he was wearing,
   To cover his playmate up warm,
He stripped to his shirt, as if daring
   The spirits of evil and harm,
And all the long night he kept watching
   Alone by that horrible bed,
Till the strange little boy woke to give his friends joy,
   But the Beautiful Watcher is dead.

Rain Through the Roof.

A STORY OF WET WEATHER.

IN the night,
   When the light
Of my chamber lamp was burning
   Dim and low,
   In its glow
As a life to God returning,
I heard the jolly jingle of the water spirit's feet;
Driven from the blotted heavens, they were merry
     in the street;
They were bounding from the pavement, they were
     dancing on the roof

Of my little city cottage—and it is not waterproof;
    For there came, my soul to flutter,
    Through a crevice in the gutter,
To our dormitory flooring, near the bed whereon I sat,
    Drops of water, dirty brown;
    Saying as they hastened down—
        Skit, scat, pit, pat,
      Pat-ter, scat-ter, skit-ter, scat-ter;
        Pit, pat, scat-ter, scat;
The voices of the water made a melody like that!

    In my shirt I sat to shiver
    As the sedges by a river;
Till my lady-love, awakened from her slumber by
      the sound,
    Started, screaming from her pillow,
    As a mermaid from a billow,
Sadder than a weeping willow by a stream of water
      bound,
    Started screaming "What's the matter?"
    And the rain said—pit-ter, pat-ter,
'Tis the water-witches' revel, you will certainly be
      drowned,
      Pe-ter, pat-ter, skit, scat,
      Pat-ter, pe-ter, pit, pat,
Skit-ter, scat-ter, pe-ter, pat-ter, skit, scat, scat.

    Then her courage overtook her,
    For the sudden fear that shook her

Flew before her radiant reason; and these words
    she spake to me—
  "By the orbs of love that twinkle,
  'Tis a melancholy sprinkle;
  I am as a periwinkle in some cavern of the sea."
  But I answered, "Love, how silly:
  'Tis a thought that makes me chilly,
You shall be my water-lily!" and she laughed
    melodiously,
  Till a demon from the gutter—
  I might weep the words to utter—
At my lily spat a sputter; saying most maliciously,
  At her, drat her, pe-ter, scat-ter,
  Skit, scat, pit, pat,
  Skit-ter, scat-ter, pit, pat, scat, scat, scat.

  Up my most indignant beauty
  Started to her noble duty;
Leapt into her little slippers, and with hasty feet
    along
  From the haunt of slumber starting,
  As a sheeted ghost departing,
Kitchenward, went almost darting, for 'twas passion
    made her strong;
  Went, and brought to suit her wishes
  Pails and kettles, pans and dishes,
Till we both were wet as fishes, with our work the
    drops among,
  Then with faces kindly touching,

'Neath a broad umbrella crouching,
Like two fairies 'neath a mushroom, to the water spirits' song,
By the fire we sat and listened, most attentively and long,
And I laughed to hear this changing in the sounding of their song—
Dip, dap, drip, drop,
Slip, slap, slush, slop,
Dip-per, dap-per, drip-per, drop-per,
Slip-per, slap-per, slush-er, slop-per,
Slip, slap, slop.

Spake my love while we were warming,
"Well, if novelty be charming,
We have found it to remember, *in this world of tears,* my man,
Such a world I never sat in;
'Tis enough to drown a rat in;
Just run down and let the cat in; shift that bucket, pail, and pan.
I declare, this tub is brimming;
Sure, if sleep my eyes were dimming,
I should dream that I was swimming
In about it, like a swan,
For last night I dreamt of tripping
Through a storm of something slipping
From the heavens, just like dripping
From a goose; and thus it ran—

Slip, slap, skit, scat,
Drip, drop, pit, pat,
Slip-per, slop-per, skit-ter, scat-ter,
Drip-per, drap-per, pit-ter, pat-ter,
Fit, fat-ter, fit, fat,
And my spirit in its vision heard a melody like that;"
Spake my little dripping dreamer as beside the fire
we sat.

The Orphan's City, Ashley Hill, Bristol.

STRAIGHT as the tall poplar's shadow,
   Lying on the bright green meadow,
Westward, from my chamber window,
   On a flowery mantled hill,
Stands a city, that was neither
Built by kings or Commons either;
But the soul of one believer,
   Working out the Master's will,
Was the builder of that city
   On the "flowery mantled" hill.

It has neither spires nor towers,
It is peopled with strange flowers,
Brought from Sorrow's saddest bowers,
   Snatched from poverty and sin

By the graces of the city,
Faith, Hope, Charity, and Pity,
But 'tis Love's twin-sister Pity,
　　Bears the drooping blossoms in;
From the saddest haunts of sorrow
　　Bears the tender blossoms in.

Tenderlings, with tear-worn faces;
Wany waifs from desert places,
Wanting what the grave embraces,
　　Wanting father's knees to climb;
Wanting mother's hands to press them,
Mother's gentle voice to bless them,
Wanting angels to caress them,
　　From the labyrinths of crime;
And a mighty love to teach them
　　How to "make their lives sublime."

So a spirit mercy-gifted,
Out of Heaven's bosom drifted,
As the odours that are lifted
　　When the winds and roses part.
And it raised the flowerets pining,
Till God saw their graces shining,
And their fond affections twining
　　Round their benefactor's heart;
In the city of the orphans,
　　Round a new-found father's heart.

Tell me, O ye carping, clever,
Philosophic scoffers, whether
That your goddess Reason ever
   Has by love or duty led
You, in all the world's history,
Thus to build its crown of glory;
Answer, sophist sage and hoary,
   From your souls by faith unfed,
When did Science, *in this manner*,
   Give two thousand orphans bread.

To the sceptic walking creedless,
As a pilgrim staff and reedless,
Through the valley, heaven heedless,
   I will say and sing it still,
'Tis a city that was neither
Built by kings or Commons either;
But the soul of one believer,
   Working out the Master's will,
Was the builder of that city,
   Up the "flowery mantled hill.

Under a Cloud.

THERE are a thousand mysteries in life,
   And this is one of them: That youth should be
Lifted from evil and the battle strife,
   While age, full ripe for death as some old tree,
Outlives a hundred storms that rent apart
And cleft the branches from their parent's heart.

I cannot help what course my fancies take,
   Since that dread day wherein my boy fell down
So dead asleep that he no more may wake
   Till God shall raise him from "the silent town,"
And Mercy lead him from his mouldy bed—
I only know my thoughts are with the dead.

My stricken soul is as a bird that haunts
   Some sacred cypress, when the storm severe
Blows on its rocking boughs, and darkness plants
   Her banner o'er my world, in which I hear
No welcome voice, nought but my hope's farewell,
The wail of women, and a tolling bell.

Under this cloud I smite a painful lyre,
   Because it was a cruel death to die,
Crushed* by the iron steed whose heart is fire.
   No warning voice, no token, no good-bye,

* At Swindon Station, April 16th, 1872.

To the green world above his dreamless bed,
Only one groan, and then my boy fell dead.

I wandered over the violeted heath,
   Seeking faint solace where spring glories sprung,
The plaintive wail came from a bramble wreath,
   Of a sad mavis mourning for its young;
I did not dream till then that there could be
One waif in life so far from joy as me.

Save one that did the dreadful news impart,
   Whose painful pen hath made us sadly wise,
Unhappy Mary of the tender heart,
   And a pale mother with wild haggard eyes,
Weeping warm tears because she knew 'twas vain,
To weep for her dead child beyond all pain.

Sweet is the sympathy of things that grieve,
   I cannot tell you why a fancy odd
Should sing to cheer me, but I do believe
   That minstrel bird was sent by nature's God
To chant in our Gethsemane of pain
A dirge of sorrow for our darling slain.

I know a world through which I came too fast,
   A love-lumed Queendom, glorious, green, and
      grand;
But now it is a graveyard called the past,
   Wherein the wrecks of hope's high castles stand,
All tumbling to decay, and ruined halls
With memories ivy-bound on their gray walls.

I would go down unto that realm once more,
    But that my present is a dungeon dark,
Wherein I grope but may not find the door,
    So that my soul is as a captive lark,
Shot down with broken wings from heaven's gate,
Waiting for balm that may be brought too late.

Time is not now to me what time hath been;
    I know my hope is dead, but I exist
In a care-conquered state, two worlds between,
    And all my future lies enthralled in mist.
What shall I do that I may win heart's ease,
Except this storm doth beat me to my knees?

Break out, O light! let this black cloud be rent,
    That I may search the diamonded skies,
To find the pathway from this mangled tent
    Of a free spirit hid by tearful eyes,
For I am as a frightened child whose scream
Leaps in the midnight from a ghastly dream.

One blessed ray from a pale, trembling star,
    Creeps softly down, pure as the balmy glow
Of chastened sheen from heaven's gate ajar,
    Tell me, sweet Mercy, for I long to know,
Is it to light me from sad sorrow's cave,
Or wake a daisy on poor Willie's grave?

Hymen's Acid.

MY love is cross, and so am I;
   I can't be happy, though I try;
I long to bid the world good-bye,
    But cannot part with Polly;
Grief hangs her banner on my face;
My household gods are out of grace;
And home is such a dreary place;
    'Tis all through loving Polly.

How shall I break this icy wall
That holds my idol in its thrall?
I must not let my manhood fall,
    Nor bend my pride to Polly.
And yet, my heart, I dare not scorn
The sighs that 'scape her lips forlorn,
How shall I kiss away the thorn
    That pains the heart of Polly?

I cannot work; I cannot rest,
With this sweet sorrow in my breast;
I almost hate what I love best;
    'Tis just the same with Polly.
I wish my love was frank and free,
As the old love that came to me
When Cupid shot my spirit free
    From the blue eyes of Polly.

Before I climb my chamber stairs,
I want to bear the cross she bears;
I cannot pray my evening prayers,
   Except I pray for Polly.
For if I pray, how shall I plead?
Alas! in this dear hour of need,
A blessed thing it were indeed,
   If all was well with Polly.

I will defy my heart's desire;
I will not to my bed retire;
Here will I wait afront the fire,
   To hear the call of Polly.
While that she lies in bed alone,
I will not let her hear me groan;
I will be dumb as marble stone,
   And try to conquer Polly.

How shall I end this trouble sore?
'Twas twelve o'clock, but now 'tis four;
It was my fault, a little more
   Than 'twas the fault of Polly.
But how shall I this silence break,
When she should be the first to speak?
I cannot for forgiveness seek,
   Except I bend to Polly.

When time for rest was drawing near,
She used to say, "Come on, my dear;"

Yet she is gone, and I am here;
  'Twas very wrong of Polly.
My joys are all a blighted crop,
My care a hag that comes to stop,
My life is one great acid drop;
  'Tis all through loving Polly.

Ah! sweet and sour together mixed;
I almost wish my fate was fixed;
I am such pain and bliss betwixt;
  Shall I go up to Polly?
Come on, cold feet, her touch may thrill;
Love wins the fight, against my will,
The road to heaven is uphill,
  'Tis just the same to Polly.

The Funeral.

I REMEMBER it was winter,
  And that icy-fingered printer
Left his hideous impressions on the faces of the poor,
  That we met while sadly strolling
  Through the city, to the tolling
Of the Sabbath bells, extolling Heaven's love and Mercy's store
  But I heeded not their wooing,
  For I knew that I was going

To be parted, and for ever, from a friend beloved of
    yore;
        Parted by a woe devasting,
        O'er my life dark shadows casting,
And a grief that will be lasting, till my pilgrimage
    is o'er.

        Sadly, with a load I carried,
        In the city street I tarried—
Tarried wan and terror-stricken by a flock of ghastly
    things,
        Beetle black and cavern-chested,
        Raven-plumed and sable-crested,
That about his dwelling rested, with their heavy
    velvet wings
        Drooping dustward, in the manner
        Of a breeze-forsaken banner;
Ah, I know what they come after in a world where
    pleasure stings;
        So my heart was terror-stricken,
        As the autumn leaves that sicken
When their fellows fall to quicken with the life of
    future springs.

        Then the voice of anguish stifled,
        In a temple pleasure-rifled,
Bursting from its sanctuary, smote a swift respond-
    ing string,
        In my bosom comfort craving.
        But I listened to the raving,

To the wild unholy raving of a strange imagining,
  Till my reason sank affrighted,
  And my sadder spirit sighted
Through her misty turret windows what awoke my fear to sing:
  Then a taloned Trouble tore me
  On the sin-damned orb that bore me
As the cortège came before me of the sin-begotten King.

  Clouds of crape, with fearful faces
  Peering from their black embraces,
Melancholy monsters rolling o'er my heart that bled in vain;
  And Despair beside me stalking,
  Demon of the funeral talking
To my spirit, westward walking with the sable-crested train,
  Saying, "Thou shalt never meet him,
  But his mother Earth shall eat him,"
Till I called the Demon liar, but he answered thus again:
  "What is man that God should mind him,
  When the door is closed behind him,
Can thy Hope or Love unbind him—ever break his icy chain?"

  Then my Hope fell faint and cheerless,
  Till a seraph bold and fearless

Told me how a little acorn fell beneath the sudden stroke
    Of a ruthless blast that tore it
    From a parent's arms that bore it,
When an angel waiting for it hid it in a dusty cloak;
    Whence it blossomed, green and glorious,
    As a soul o'er death victorious:
Then the coffin of the acorn was the cradle of the oak.
    So the mighty Father taketh
    Tender care of all He maketh,
From the meanest mite He waketh, to a spirit in its yoke.

To the World.

THERE is a wrong beneath the sun,
  A wrong of fellow men,
With which I dare in battle run
  That weapon called a pen;
My pen indeed a puny thing,
  Yet if my aim I miss,
Still for the Right I hold the ring,
  And charge the world like this:

You cheer the man that wins the prize;
  You laud and call him great;
But he that fails in what he tries
  Ye trample 'neath your feet:

The man that fails to hit his mark,
  Although his aim was high,
Ye hurry to oblivion dark:
  In mercy tell me why?

No matter what our spheres may be,
  If there's a goal to find,
One runs the race triumphantly,
  The thousands lag behind:
The course may be the same in length,
  But some Dame Fortune starts,
And there are some with little strength,
  That carry broken hearts.

To him that does not want your cheers
  A thousand cheers you give,
On him that fails you pile your sneers,
  Until 'tis pain to live.
Why are ye guilty of such deeds?
  I scorn your cruel plan:
Why don't you help the thing that needs,
  And cheer the proper man?

The Old Pauper's Song.

OH, joy is a tide that ebbs and flows,
Whether or whence God only knows!
The poor man's cross is a pain to bear,
But the crown of glory is the yoke of care.
I have seen happiness far from wealth,
And misery eating a rich man's health;
I have worshipped a rose whose roots ran down
Through the roof of a grave in the silent town.
There's many a cheek, where bright smiles glow,
That do not spring from the heart I trow.
Oh, Joy is a tide that ebbs and flows,
Whither or whence God only knows!

Oh, man is little and God is great!
Summer lies dead beneath my feet;
The rose is withered, the lark is dumb,
The swallows are flown from the wrath to come;
Spring will wake and summer will smile,
But what of the poor that starve the while?
The spirit of love has sent them food,
But the evil of man is mixed with good.
Self holds the sieve while angels pour,
And what cares Self for the hungry poor?
Do the winds for the leaves beneath my feet?
Oh, man is little and God is great!

The swallows were wise, but the robin is bold,
Look up, little souls that long for gold,

He is flinging me down a splendid proof
Of the Father's care from my cottage roof;
Except you feel you never can see
What that love carol is worth to me;
But you may reckon, of course you can,
What you are worth to your fellow man;
How do you gather? and what do you give?
'Twill be harder to die than it is to live.
Ah me! that robin has made me bold—
Look up, little souls that starve for gold.

Oh, bride of my heart, come hither to me,
For I have a song to sing to thee:
The year of our life is in its wane,
And our pathway home is a thorny lane.
We have laughed together when our hearts were light;
We have wept together in care's black night;
We've fought for each other in the days that are past;
We have lived for each other, let us love to the last.
We may meet Death in a pauper's ward,
But if Heaven is near 'twill not be hard;
I ask no Heaven that holds not thee—
Bride of my soul, come thither with me.

A Book.

My lady's face is as a book
  Whereon I love with love to look,
   Because I read the golden lore
Of Truth and Faith upon it blent,
   Such as I never read before,
That happy hour when it was sent
To make my life magnificent.

An open book it is to me,
Revealing half my destiny,
   And for my care a pleasant charm;
My dearest thoughts it doth entrance;
   It is to save my soul from harm,
A shrine from whence her virtues glance
With more than mortal elegance.

A joy it is much joy above,
To read it by the lamps of love,
   That in thought's palace windows shine
Ah! that to me is joy indeed;
   But there's a pleasure more divine
My lady will to me concede;
It is to kiss the book I read.

Sonnets on Chatterton's Church, Bristol.

WHAT hast thou seen, O pilgrim! in the valley?
    What hast thou found from this great world
  of ours,
Rising more glorious or majestically
    That this tall temple, made of sculptor flowers,
By Art triumphant, and her high born ally,
    Seraphic Genius? 'Tis a palace vast,
On which I gaze with beauty-loving eyes,
    Because I know 'twas raised in ages past,
For the great Queen of Hope's pure Paradise,
    Soul-saving Love. The swift-winged angel light,
That leaps from Heaven's window, lustre shedding,
    Hath not descended from her native skies,
Or glanced from glory on a grander wedding,
    Of airy elegance with massy might.

It is not like a temple made by men;
    A man within its compass barely seems
More than a miner mole that makes its den
    In a tall mountain's foot. The grandest dreams
Of painter poets flash from shining sheets
Of saint emblazoned crystal. Beauty greets
You in this hall of Death. When that the door
    Doth shut you in another world you tread,
Where arborescent monsters from the floor,
    Shoot to the ribbed roof, whereon they spread

Their ravelled branches till that roof appears
    The haunt of spirits watching o'er the dead
That slumber in a sepulchre of years,
    Wherein we muse by its famed founder's bed.

As a full moon, in the blue heavens dancing
    Among the stars with harmony sublime,
Soars from her silver couch with smiles enchancing,
    Shall this fair fabric from the grasp of time
    Rise with replenished splendour to the chime
Of holy bells; and melodies entrancing,
    Shall float above this vale of tears and crime,
    Up unto God like the glad gushing rhyme
Of bards who see the golden age advancing,
    When Sharon's Rose shall bloom in every clime
Beneath the blessing sun; then angels glancing
    From their high home shall bless this altar prime,
As man is blest when mercy doth depart
Out from the soul of God, in heaven's heart.

In these dear days this earth shall not be damned
    By a dire dearth of love. Love shall with joy
Open her palace doors that now be slammed,
    Defying entrance to the "marv'lous boy."
He in the cold outside stands carved in stone
    Like some unshriven soul. He sang for bread,
And, starving, died. We to his ghost instead
    Bequeath the granite that shall not atone
For our forefathers' shame. What deed were worse
    Than this exclusion from his dearest fane,

These are the days when juries round a corse
   Of him that dares seek Death say 'twas insane.
What then of Chatterton? forgive his sin,
Open the temple doors, and let him in.

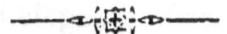

How Mary Died.

I COULD not tell you, if I were to try,
   How that it was our darling Mary died;
Sometimes I fancy that she did not die,
   But that she faded as the stars that glide
Out softly from the darkness, to be lost
   In the full blaze of a grand summer day—
   Yes that was how her sweet soul sailed away.
I cannot tell the pain our parting cost,
   Nor name the value, which is known to God,
Of all the shining pearls that trembling Love
   Dropt from her palace windows, when the rod
Of sorrow smote our hearts, but high above
   This night wherein my stricken spirit pines
   I look for Mary where the day blaze shines.

Resignation.

THE Hand that buried Moses
   Has laid my babe to sleep,
Among the faded roses
   His guardian angels keep;
And so sweetly it reposes
   That my love should never weep.

So kindly was it taken
   From evil, that I know,
With confidence unshaken,
   Whatever storm may blow,
I am not long forsaken
   Where tears of sorrow flow.

I saw His angels leading
   My darling from its play;
Low on my bosom bleeding
   A little while it lay;
Then, while my love was pleading,
   It smiled and went away.

Once when my soul was knitting
   Past joy with present care,
A flock of dark thoughts, flitting
   Like swallows through the air,
Came, and I saw Death sitting
   In Baby's empty chair.

And that was all through grieving,
　Sure love will have its way!
Fond memory, too, keeps weaving
　Fresh love knots every day.
Still, in my sad heart heaving,
　Bold Faith shall sing and say—

"The Hand that buried Moses
　Hath laid my babe to sleep,
Among the faded roses
　His guardian angels keep;
And so sweetly it reposes
　That my love should never weep."

Fame.

FAME is the tinkle of a bell,
　Suspended in a crumbling tower,
Of a strange realm 'twixt heaven and hell,
　Where care has blighted every flower.
He that the steep ascent would climb,
To pull a peal must murder time;
For all the stairs are thick with stains
Of blood, and tears, and wasted brains.
Fame is not worth the hunter's pains
Until he dies, then eager friends
Will crown his ghost to make amends.

Blighted Hopes.

"OVER the billows of life's troubled main,"
    Sang a fair maid, with her eyes full of glee,
"Christmas the merry is coming again,
    Bearing a burden of pleasure for me."
What did it bring her? A tear-spangled garland
    Lies on the roof of a newly-made tomb:
May her sweet spirit above the blue star-land
    Warble love carols in melody's home.

"Weep not, my darling," a fond mother cried;
    "Come to my heart, and glad news I will tell:
Home with the morning star over the tide
    Father is coming, and all will be well."
Why does she weep? 'Twas the cruel wind snarling,
    Up ran the breaker and down went the ship,
Where is the hope that she offered her darling?
    Why was it dashed from humanity's lip?

Why? 'Tis a secret that death may reveal—
    God only knows why our hopes should depart;
There's never a day but what cometh to steal
    A love-cherished flower away from the heart.
Low in the dust of the paths we have travelled
    Skeletons lie of the hopes that were ours;
And, though our sorrows with pleasures are ravelled
    Memory weeps for her fair, fallen flower.

Here in my bower of holly and bay,
  Why should I whistle to keep away Fear?
Under the mistletoe pearly and gay,
  Why should I mourn in this happy New Year?
Tis not that friendship or love has been slighted,
  Nor for the time that flew merry and fast;
But I must muse on the hopes that are blighted—
  Blighted by Death in the year that is past.

A Christmas Idyl.

Crowned with holly,
  Hale and jolly,
Even as in years away,
See, our snow-robed friend is hither—
Heaven only knows from whither—
Make him welcome while you may.
  Care is vanished,
  Self is banished;
Love is queen of the world to-day.

  Bells are ringing,
  Bards are singing
Happy songs like birds in May;
And we all to gladness waking
Revel in a sweet love-making;

Hearts are warmed, and fond lips say:
    Glad we see you,
    Merry be you;
Love is queen of the world to-day.

    Up and greet her,
    Out and meet her;
By the beggar in thy way
In thy pleasure pass not heedless;
For the best are never needless
Of some want for which to pray.
    Buy a blessing
    Worth possessing;
Love is queen of the world to-day.

    In the mellow
    Primrose yellow
Softened lamp-fire's golden ray,
Parted friends, each other greeting,
Bless the merry Christmas meeting,
Pleasant memories wake to play;
    All exclaiming,
    And proclaiming,
Love is queen of the world to-day.

    Out with sorrow,
    Till to-morrow;
In with pleasure, and for aye;
In the way you went to gain it
Give it; so thou shalt retain it,

Pure and perfect from decay,
    To the ending
    Of life's spending;
Love is queen of the world to-day.

    Hunger scampers
    From her hampers;
Know you where it goes to stay?
Where the widow's child lies dreaming
Happy dreams of dainties teeming,
And the angel's roundelay:
    Up and find her,
    Just remind her
Love is queen of the world to-day.

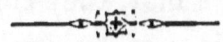

Bertha.

A TALE OF THE AMERICAN WAR.

AWAKE! Awake! for freedom's sake
    The hour is come, and God shall take
Sure vengeance on the foes of right,
For manhood's tyrants in the fight
That will not bend to Lincoln's star
    Shall perish by the sword they drew,
And by the blaze of ruthless war
    Be smitten for the strife they grew;

As autumn leaves by wind and flood
Fall stricken, they shall fall in blood;
It is their choice, it is their will,
To die in the defence of ill.

So in the North the cry, "To arms!"
Rang thunder loud; and eager swarms
Leapt from the lap of Peace, to save
The nation's life. Grey parents gave
Their willing sons to stem the shock
Of war begun; forth with his flock
The pastor from the temple came,
For manhood's right, in freedom's name;
Not by desire for conquest urged,
But for Columbia's banner purged
From slav'ry's blot, they come to fight;
And for the love of human right;
It is their will, their mind, their mood,
To die in the defence of good.

Peace to the land where war abode
   Again returns—the slave is free;
   And young Columbia o'er the sea,
Flings to the flying winds abroad,
A thousand banners 'neath the skies
Pure as his mother England flies.
But there's of love a dreadful dearth;
Not half so kind as mother earth,
Are all that have outlived the strife,
For labour's right, and manhood's life.

The God that in her bosom lives
So full her children's crime forgives,
That where the strife hath fiercest been
Her grasses wear their grandest green;
And where her warriors' graves abound
The fairest of her jewels are found.

Beneath a fair Virginny sky,
By a dear home to Richmond nigh,
   Reposing on the garden sward,
In the blest hour of day's decline,
When spirits for communion pine,
   Three sunny summers afterward,
Thus of the war for freedom's sake,
Face unto face two brothers spake.
The time had been when these were foes,
But when the strife was nigh its close
A strange event made friends of both,
And they to love were nothing loth.
Why do they start? What sudden force
Of sound hath hushed their deep discourse?

Down by the garden's farthest bound
   There was a poisoned water well;
   And through its mouth a negro's yell
Shot with a sudden piercing sound;
He was among a band that toiled
To purge the flood of waters spoiled:
What have they found they would not find,
And in their terror left behind?

From the well bottom deep, and dank,
A corpse was lifted to the bank;
And through a southern soldier's vest,
A rusty dagger in his breast
Lay driven deep; within that sheath
Who was it drove the blade for death?
When was it done? why was the deed?
Was such a doom a soldier's meed?
What was the name he bore about
The world before his soul went out?
He that would find the answers hid
Should with my minstrel at his bid
Come to the time of war along,
And learn the story from his song.

Edgar, my hero, in the van
With Lincoln's host, a noble man,
Swift to the field must haste away,
 And well he wears a soldier's look,
Although it is his marriage day,
 And he hath left sweet Bertha Brooke,
Weeping beside the temple door,
Lest he, to her, should come no more.
For they have loved long years, and now
The bridegroom on her virgin brow
Hath left behind his parting kiss,
 Beside his wealth of love profound;
And must she live his love to miss?
It is a thought which frightens bliss,
 Her heart is trembling to the sound

Of War awake, the trumpets blare;
The roll of drums; the banners flare;
The scream of fifes, the heavy tramp
Of legions marching to the camp;
In dread array, with ring of steel;
God! what a horrid bridal peal.

Alas! for such a wedding-day;
Led by her maids, she turns away,
And to her rural home afar,
Flies as a dove the demon War—
Affrighted from his presence foul,
And he, the idol of her soul,
Is gone, is gone, perchance to die;
Ah! now to Love and Hope good-bye,
So sang the Fears she strove to chase,
While tears were streaming her fair face;
But now her home in sight appears,
And she must wipe away her tears;
In Ravenhall there is a room
Where she will wait to know her doom.

A wealthy merchant was her sire,
   But he was with her mother dead,
And she had seen long years expire
   Since they went home with death to bed.
Her guardian was a kinsman kind,
A man of wealth and taste refined,
Who loved her for his sister flown,
As if the child were all his own.

Thus from sweet youth to maiden prime
Ran with her life the stream of time;
Alas! that care should stir the stream,
Or fate dispel her young heart's dream.
The old man died, and she was left
Of all her earthly kin bereft;
Then, sorrow taught, poor Bertha prayed
The mighty Father God for aid.
That aid how needful! There was one
Who strove to win what Edgar won;
But more than love her wealth he sought,
 And when she firmly answered, No,
Thy passion is not worth my thought,
 He said, Beware! I am thy foe,
If man save me shall call thee wife,
I am his curse and thine through life.

Was it because his vow he kept
Fair Bertha bent her brow and wept?
She drops a letter from her hand,
 The words are not from Edgar's pen;
It doth her instant flight command;
 His foe, Red Ralph, is in the glen,
A troop of rebel horse he leads,
And dares to do the worst of deeds;
'Tis said the Union ranks he fled,
Because a comrade's blood he shed;
That deep he played, and deeply drank,
Till deep in vice and debt, he sank;

That in a haunt where gamblers meet,
To win a stake he strove to cheat,
Then words arose, and swords were drawn,
To sheathe again, until 'twas dawn;
But ere the dawn, the sentry found
A soldier's corpse, with a wide wound,
Stretched on the pavement damp and red,
And Ralph a traitor vanishèd.

A raid to-night on Ravenhall
 The rebels ride; and to their ire,
Enwrapt in flames the house shall fall;
But in the hours before the fire
Begins to burn, my rival's dove
Shall fly afar on wings of love;
Ah! well; 'tis well; for he will know
Whose hand it was that smote the blow.
I told her he to death was nigh,
In Richmond; thence to prove the lie
Fate speed the fool. Where stays my slave
That bore the letter? Curse the knave;
He should be here this time before;
By God I'll lash his back to gore:
If he comes not I count the cost
Will be five hundred dollars lost;
His mother was against her will
More than my slave; if I do spill
His Creole blood it will be mine,
And slaves are slaves by right divine;

Thus as he rode for ruin's sake
His thoughts the reckless raider spake.

Home from the field with brief respite
My hero rides in haste; for he
Had read the story of that night,
When Ralph the raider savagely
Laughed like a demon in the glare
Of fire-fiends dancing in the air,
That flung their banners red and wide
Over the shrine from whence his bride
Sped on the fretful feet of fear
To seek her lord; yet he is here,
With feature white as marble stone,
Between the roofless walls alone.

Alive or dead; where, whence, and how
   Shall Edgar seek his virgin bride?
These are the thoughts that rack his brow,
   As from the scene he turns aside;
All the long days of his respite
From war he sought his soul's delight,
Till by despair his hopes were slain;
Then to the war he rode again,
And where more fiercely raged the strife,
He taunted Death to take his life.

Was he protected by a charm,
Or by a guardian angel's arm?

'Twas strange that he should scathless come
From the jaws of death, at the roll of the drum;
And with the living be counted one,
A unit left of thousands gone;
Gone where? Ah! "there's the rub," we must
Ask God, and not our mother dust.
Few were his words, his thoughts were more;
Never a smile the warrior wore,
Where beams of mirth were wont to play,
As sun-gleams dance on flowers of May;
Despair had set his seal instead,
His heart was as a tomb of lead,
Wherein his dearest hopes lay hid
From Love, till mem'ry raised the lid,
And then sad Love would weep in vain,
Until the lid was closed again.

Of all the night the blackest hour
   Is not the worst, for from its gloom
Fair rosy morn breaks out in flower,
   And light, from darkness, leaps abloom;
So angel-lifted from the heart
Shall sorrow's deepest shades depart;
Thus in an hour by heaven sent
A comrade came to Edgar's tent,
And as when friends each other meet,
After some salutations sweet
Were interchanged for friendship's sake,
'Twas thus the brother warrior spake.

Edgar, my friend, I heard you say
You want a help; along my way
Toward your tent I found your need,
A splendid fellow you'll concede,
A slave he was, but has forsook
His bonds, as fish escape the hook,
Pray let me introduce him—look.

A swarthy lad, who wore a fair
Soft shining cap of raven hair
In curls above his shapely brow,
Made his appearance and his bow;
His eyes were rolling orbs of light,
  His lips lay open as a bell,
Exhibiting twin rows of white
  Teeth like the chips of cockleshell,
A nose his brow and chin betwixt
Was Ham's and Japhet's intermixt;
The features of his face were kind
And a true index of his mind;
That mind oppress'd with wrong and grief,
Such is the stranger's sketch in brief.

Strange are the ways of God, or fate,
  Which will you say? in all but name
Are not these myths our minds create—
  Chance, Fate, and Providence, the same?
The Great Unknown to Edgar's tent
Hath led the man the raider sent,

Laden with falsehood long before,
To Ravenhall; 'twas he that bore
Ralph's letter to the virgin bride,
And he hath slipped his bonds beside;
Now, from his lips shall Edgar know
Whose was the hand that gave the blow.

What man of all the Southern host
   Armed for oppression rank and rife
Is he my hero loveth most,
   And fears to injure in the strife?
Alas! for Love; it is the brave
Son of his mother in the grave.
One moment of a dreadful day
Brought Claude and Edgar in the fray
Face unto face; and then they saw
In a brief glance with kindred awe
Each other's ire; but love forbade,
And turned aside each brother's blade
On other foes, too quickly found,
Among the madder mass around;
But when the fight was "lost, and won,"
   A summer moon in the blue field
Of heaven, like a silver shield,
   Above my wounded hero shone.

Alas! alas! for Bertha Brooke,
How can my wounded hero look?
   He frets within a prison foul,

Where starving braves of death are glad,
Because that they are hunger mad;
  And armed sentries on them scowl :
How now can Claude for Edgar care
While keepers steal their captive's fare?
  His brother's doom he does not know
Till days are dead; then to his farm
He brings to nurse a bandaged arm,
  Broke by a hostile bullet's blow;
More than his love expects to win
What will he find that home within?

Beneath his roof, in mortal guise,
  The sweetest soul love ever sent,
  To make the world magnificent,
Grasped by the hand of fever lies;
And when the fury shook her frame,
He heard his brother Edgar's name,
Wild as a troubled sea-bird's screech,
Break through the burning gates of speech.
And while they watched her bed beside,
To see the fever flame subside,
The story of her woe severe
His gentle Lady told; and ere
One half the tender task was done
His brother's foe became his own,
And with a sigh, he spake, alas!
That falsehood foul should come to pass.

Why should he now his wrath conceal?
  At once for love and beauty's sake,
  He will the road to Richmond take,
Nor wait at home his wound to heal;
Where Bertha sought her love in vain
Before the time, he will again.
It is the rival chieftains' plan
To change their captives, man for man.
And then! and then! the thought was sweet,
He will his brother's care entreat;
If that his chief should grant the boon
The bride shall see her husband soon.
Zenobia and his lady fair
Will for his new-found sister care
Till his return, with Edgar free
From prison bonds; but who is she
That by his lady bends above
The virgin bride with looks of love?

Zenobia was in years before
The slave of Ralph, and something more
By him, against her will, she bore
A son, that broke from slav'ry's thrall
When he was sent to Ravenhall,
She for her hate of Ralph was sold
Unto a better master's gold,
When half the beauty of her frame
Was wrecked to lust that knew no shame,

And still she wore the grace and mien
That should adorn proud Ethop's queen;
But in her eyes bright passion shone
Because her thoughts were of her son:
Ah! when will time that vengeance give
For which she seems alone to live?

The day is past, the hour is late,
Through Claude the planter's mansion gate
That unto them is open wide,
A band of armèd horsemen ride.
To them his absence shall not be
A bar to hospitality;
For she that in his absence rules
Is one of nature's rarest jewels;
A woman true, as minted gold,
She will her lord's good name uphold;
Whether the war be wrong or right
'Tis with the South her kinsmen fight,
But there is one among the train
That will not mount his steed again.

The feast is spread, the lamps are lit,
The guests around the table sit;
And laden with the wine that cheers
Zenobia in their 'midst appears.
Why does she in her duty start
   As if an arrow from the bow
Of Death was planted in her heart?
     Perchance the raider Ralph may know;

For when his eyes and hers were paired
Two evil spirits sat and stared
Upon each other; and the glance
Of hatred from her countenance,
Flashed as a flame of hell upon
The sensual sire of her lost son.
It was a look that seemed to blast
His lusty soul, that shrank aghast;
Despite the answering look he gave
To her, no more his splendid slave.

It is a glorious night; the moon,
Out of the jewelled heaven, pours
A flood of glory through the doors
   That open from the fair saloon
To the verandah; there the beams
Of laughing light, in radiant streams,
Rain, as a shower of silver spears,
On a gay group of banqueteers,
But who is he that deeply drinks
Until the goddess Reason sinks
        Drowned in the cup
        He lifteth up,
And his wild tongue begins to wag
   Of battle, thunder, trumpets, guns,
And Glory, that infamous hag,
   The bride of Havock, Wisdom shuns?
Ah who is he whose bluster grew
Till his affronted friends withdrew

Soul-sickened with his language foul?
'Tis Ralph, the champion of the bowl.
There let him bask in Cyntha's fire
He will not rise at their desire;
For when expressed 'twas he that said
I am not of the night afraid;
Ralph does not trust to God his life;
This trusty dagger in the strife
Shall be my friend if friend I need,
And I am ready for the deed:
What wonder then if in disgust
They leave the boaster to his trust?

Bring me the life-blood of the vine,
And let me fill my veins with wine,
He cries, and lo! at his commands
Zenobia in his presence stands.
Not with that look she wore when first
She came with cheer to quench their thirst;
Her voice is tender-toned and sad,
Because her thoughts are of the lad,
And if her words confess her hate,
How can she hope to learn his fate—
That hate which in her bosom gnaws,
Lies hidden as a tiger's claws
Are, till the furry-footed beast
Tears with delight its bloody feast.

* * * *

The lights that o'er the banquet shone
   Within their crystal shrines expire;
The guests are from the table gone,
   It is the Wizard Sleep's desire.

And quietly, with a snow-white face,
   Beautiful Bertha on her bed
Lies fever left in Sleep's embrace,
   The image of an angel dead.

To tend her wants her sister kind
   Hovers the prostrate form above;
Long hath she left her guest behind
   To do the gentle deeds of love.

'Tis well for them they do not know
   Poor Bertha's foe is of the band;
'Tis better for the knave below
   That noble Claude is not at hand.

Too well hath proud Zenobia hid
   All knowledge of his presence foul;
She stands before him at the bid
   Of love that thrills her hapless soul.

It is her darling son she seeks,
   She does not know of his escape;
It is a mother's love that speaks
   Unto the brute in human shape.

In language meek the proud quadroon
    Her question garbs; "Ah!" he replies,
"If from my lips I grant the boon,
    I ask a joy from thine likewise."

The meaning of his words she caught,
    And this befitting answer gave;
"Once all my love was thine for naught,
    For I to thee was more than slave.

What boon from me dost thou desire?
    Hast thou not robbed my life of joy?
How dare thy lips to mine aspire?
    In mercy tell me of my boy.

Can I forget that night of old
    When from his arms about me bound
You tore me for my price in gold?
    Or lick the hand that gave the wound?

It was my blood, my bones, my flesh,
    And I was thine while thou hast need;
Thy answer tears the wound afresh:
    I hate thee for the damnèd deed."

The demon Lust his eyes within,
    Sat staring on her beauty, till
He caught her hands, his aim to win,
    And spake these words to gain his will:

"Come, pretty devil, let me lie
　　My head on thy soft lap a spell;
Thou shalt from me with kisses buy
　　The tidings it is mine to sell."

She tore her body from his grasp,
　　She could not bide the demon's stare,
She left her raiment in his clasp,
　　She fled before him as a hare.

Her hut was by the garden bound,
　　Her flight was down the garden path,
He runs behind her as a hound
　　Runs for its prey with savage wrath.

Haste! haste! Zenobia; haste ahead,
　　His hand a gleaming blade contains,
And thou hast more than death to dread
　　If all the race the villain gains.

Aside to where a well mouth gapes
　　She turns her troubled life to save,
O'erleaps the danger and escapes;
　　He follows, falls, and finds a grave.

It was a well before these hours
　　From whence the household never drank,
And only for the garden flowers
　　Its flood was lifted to the bank.

His comrades in the dusky hours
   Of morn arose with wonder smote,
The well-mouth with its lip of flowers
   Betrayed no sign of him they sought.

In vain they call, in vain they look,
   From Claude the dead no answer came,
A soldier wrote upon a book,
   In the deserter's list his name.

The secret of that fearful night
   It was Zenobia's choice to hide,
And on her life it lay a blight,
   As if her tongue by Fear was tied.

Whence came that dagger in his breast?
   He fell upon it in his fall,
His was the clutch that held it best,
   And drave it through his bosom wall.

A flock of dreams to Bertha's couch
   Came the next morn on spirit wings,
Fair Fancy with her magic touch
   Awoke the maid's imaginings,

And to her in the arms of sleep
   They brought bright chains of pearls that are
Made of the tears pure virgins weep,
   When those they love go forth to war.

They hung the chains her neck around,
    They sang, " Fair lady, weep no more,
All these were by the angels found
    Aside the holy temple door."

And when the shining chains were hung
    About the maid, they smote the chords
Of tinkling lutes, and softly sung
    The tender tones of parting words.

The angel Hope in Bertha's heart
    Lay listening to their roundelay,
The watchers saw her pink lips part,
    And lo! a smile came out to play.

About her cheeks so white and wan,
    As winter snow lies on the moor,
A pretty smile of rapture ran
    From the pearl-pillared palace door.

The bridegroom, by his brother led,
    Came his dear lady love to see,
And then the happy vision fled
    Into a sweet reality.

So gentle love made haste to raise
    The fire of life on Bertha's frame;
Her eyes were kindled by its blaze,
    And through her cheeks the roses came.

Spring Joys.

AGAIN we have the spring days;
   Glad poets sing lays;
Over earth the white clouds sail summerward along.
   Again the winter snows leave;
   Lovingly the boughs weave
Bowers for the birds that sing the leaves among.

   Cheerily the blue bells
   Ring where the dew dwells;
Merrily the bees come, blithe banqueters:
   Honey they may drink till
   Daisy folds her pink frill,
And at heaven's eastern gate the angel Eve appears.

   Hark! while the lark sings
   Swift on his dark wings,
O'er the laughing brook's face swarthy swallows shoot.
   Hush! for the dove seems
   Telling us love dreams;
Violets are smiling at the forest monarch's foot.

   The squirrel, in its glee, crops
   Food on the tree tops;
Beetles flash the blades amid, butterflies above
   Caress that pretty slim rose,
   The moon-yellow primrose!
Because they love its beauty, and their duty is to love.

Sweet Philomel will sing soon
Songs to the spring moon;
With her lamp the fireworm will catch the hedge aglow:
She will light the fleet hare
To sup on dewy sweet fare;
And May will hang her white robe on the hawthorn bough.

Who will then my queen be,
Crowned 'neath the green tree,
Bessie bright or Eveline, of sweet seventeen?
Joy to my true love,
Life, hope, and new love;
Better than my old love I have never seen.

I fade, and she fades,
E'en as a tree fades
When the dead leaves drop and wet winds sigh.
I know, and she knows,
Sure as the tree grows,
We shall have a life spring in the by-and-by.

O! blessed are the spring days,
When poets sing lays;
Beautiful the world grows, the fields are angel-trod:
My soul with music gifted,
Breathes as a blossom lifted
Up from its mouldy chamber, by the awful hand of God.

To Cupid.

A BRIDAL COMPLIMENT.

WHAT hast thou been doing, Cupid,
 Since that fatal day of yore,
When I fell like some quadruped
By thine arrow smitten stupid,
And fair Fanny called me stupid
 By the shining River Tor?

I have been a restless rover,
All the rolling round world over.
I have been among the people
 Of all kingdoms, old and young;
I have danced in every steeple,
 Where a bridal bell was swung.
I have shot from beauty's windows,
 Russians, Prussians, Swedes, and Fins,
Spanish Dons, and tawny Hindoos,
 Romans, Greeks, and Mandarins.
In the shrines of elegances,
 And the damnèd dens of dearth,
I have shot my mystic lances,
 I shall conquer all the earth:
But the chief of all my battles
 And the best I ever won,
Was to lay my silken shackles
 On the Bard of Devon's Son.

Happy Bob.

A ROBIN, on a leafless tree,
  The tryant winter scorning,
Stood singing bold and merrily
  One dark November morning;
Cold, keen, and rude, loud, fierce, and chill,
  The wintry winds were blowing,
But sweet from happy Bob, and still,
  This stream of song came flowing,
      By heaven's grace
      My fate I face,
And sing to sweeten sorrow,
      Though winds may blow
      My shroud of snow
Out of the cloud to-morrow.

My soul within my breast was stirred
  To hear the pretty preacher;
And gratefully I own that bird
  Became my spirit teacher.
And thus I said, till death I meet
  I ever shall remember,
My Robin and that carol sweet
  He sang in dark November.
      For I may face
      By heaven's grace,

The cloud of grief I sob in;
    And not be less,
    When troubles press,
Than my heroic Robin.

The Meeting of the Emperors.

WHEN shall we
    Who are three
Of the mighty great and vain,
Link our gory hands again?
Much our meeting is a wonder
To the friends of peace that ponder,
Lest that we of battle fonder,
Should their dearest hopes disdain.

Soon enough the world shall know
What we speak in whispers low,
As the words of thieves that creep
Round their victims while they sleep.

When the chains we forge shall be
Fastened on humanity;
When the Russian's feet are placed
On the Ottoman disgraced;

When that Prussian Eagles glance
Death to war-exhausted France;
When that Poland's hopes expire
In the house of Hapsburg's fire,
And the plans we meet to plot
Are all stamped with steel and shot,
    Then shall we
    Mighty three
Meet again, or shall we not?

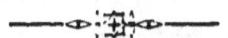

Where is Heaven?

TELL me prophet, priest, or king,
  Tell me seers or sages,
Where is Heaven? that I may sing,
  To the lives of ages;
Picture poems of that home
  Where true pleasures centre,
And that realm beyond the tomb
  Death can never enter.

Let us learn to think of this
  Ere we carp or cavil,
There is one sure path to bliss
  That we all may travel;

To the soul that truly strives,
    Ways and means are ample;
Those that beautify their lives
    Set the best example.

Sure I am, if self were less
    In our mortal leaven,
This fair world the few possess
    Might be made like heaven;
Sure am I if love was bound
    In each soul's endeavour,
Heaven sought might here be found,
    Beautiful for ever.

Weary of Life.

WEARY of life? Do you know what you are?
    Is it little or nothing to stand
Alive on the crest of this beautiful star?
    Would you fling a bright jewel out of hand,
        To please a mad whim,
        That maketh it dim,
    Are you what you might be in the land?

Weary of life? Is it nothing to ride
    Through splendour-full regions of space,

With planets that swim in the cerulean tide,
  And God taking care of our race?
      For nothing at all,
      Ere you hide in a pall—
Have you done what you might if you tried?

Weary of life? Is thy mission fulfilled,
  Hast thou finished thy share of its toil?
Shall thy epitaph be: "Here a craven lies killed?"
  Would you creep to a cave in the soil,
      And hide as a worm,
      From a pass-away storm?
Is there naught to be won from the moil?

Weary of life? Do you know you can find
  Sweet pleasure in fighting the foe?
The angels are watching, and He is all kind
  That gave thee Love's labour to do.
      For life then to arms,
      For the battle hath charms,
And thy soul shall ascend over woe.

My Garden.

I HAVE within this world of ours
A little garden filled with flowers,
Which are not as the flowers that die
When autumn clouds invade the sky.
To mine, because they wear a charm,
The winter winds shall bring no harm;
They shall not with the spring-gems fade,
Nor perish in the summer flame.
In heat or cold, in light or shade,
My garden strange is still the same;
For all the flowers within it found
Were born to bloom the whole year round.

Fair is my garden to behold,
    With borders trimmed, and portals neat,
Whereon the name is writ in gold;
    And all the flowers within are sweet—
So sweet to me because I know
It was my love that bade them blow;
And some of them came out with pain
    So often in the midnight hours,
That my warm tears did sadly rain
    Upon them; but the sweetest flowers
Of all that I have raised for love
Are those that I have wept above.

If in the night alone you sit,
    Looking the tender leaves among,

There you may see my fancies flit,
   And you may hear that mystic song
I heard the passion spirits sing
When that my flowers were opening;
And if thy thoughts to their embrace
   Thou dost consign, then shalt thou say,
This garden is a haunted place.
   Fear not, but let thy fancies play
With mine, good friend; small is thy need,
My garden is the book you read.

The Dying Hangman.

LOW on his bed, but not to rest,
   In fight with death he lay;
Of all mankind the most unblest
   That ever strove to pray
     To God, or fate,
     At Mercy's gate—
It was his judgment day.

What shapes are these that haunt his room
   To fill his soul with dread?
They are a spectre band for whom
   Judge Conscience sent ahead,
     And conjured back
     To plague and rack
Him on his dying bed.

Their throats are bound with strangling bands,
  With bursting eyes they stare;
He knows their blood is on his hands,
  With which he beats the air
    In a mad strife
    For further life—
It is his curse to bear.

With ghastly grins his bed about
  They crowd in savage glee;
They cry unto his soul, Come out,
  And thou our king shalt be;
    It was for gold
    Your soul was sold—
You murder for your fee.

Mother to Baby.

WHENCE comest thou?
  With this bright brow,
Shading blue beady eyes, beaming with love,
  Gift of God's sending me,
  Loan of His lending me,
Joy of my cottage, my dear baby dove.

  Sad is my thought,
  More than it ought,
As to my bosom I press thee with fear:
  Wilt thou grow beautiful,

Gentle and dutiful,
Up through the years of thy girlhood, my dear?

What will this fair
Soft little pair
Of pretty white hands have to do for their bread,
When I am void of breath,
Down in the house of death:
Who will be kind to them when I am dead?

Who will these feet
Hasten to meet
If in thy bosom love kindles her fire?
Will thy soul purity
Grace thy maturity?
Unto what sphere will thy spirit aspire?

Why stayest thou,
Innocent now,
Here to be tempted and tainted with sin;
Kiss me and roam away
To thy high home away,
Pilgrim, begone, ere thy sorrows begin.

Nay, my love, nay;
God let thee stay;
Darkness would follow the loss of thy smile;
Light with thy loving eyes
This wreck of Paradise;
Win thine own heaven and bless me the while.

The Red May.

When that the lanes grow shady,
　When that the winds blow sweet,
And violets bloom for my lady,
　Up at the wood-king's feet.
Come to the land where the dead lay,
　Drowned in the autumn strife,
When the powers of death made headway
　Over the flowers of life;
There while the fresh spring roses
　Break into bloom, you may see,
And stand like the prophet Moses,
　In front of a burning tree.

Out on the land where the dead lay,
　Buried in grime and mire,
A spirit of life to the red May,
　Came with a torch of fire.
First with a pink pale wan light,
　Then with a flush of flame,
As blood through the cheek of a man-mite
　Burns, so the spring fire came.
And if to the feast of roses,
　You come with the bronzy bee,
You may stand like the prophet Moses,
　In front of a burning tree.

Over the land where the dead lay,
　Up through its roots in the sod,

Sped, on the boughs of the red May,
   Flame from the torch of God!
And when the sun fire dwindled
   Down in the urn of days,
By the lamp of faith fresh kindled,
   I stood with a thought that says,
" When spring birds sing to the roses,
   And blue-bells ring for the bee,
You may stand like the prophet Moses,
   In front of a burning tree."

Out on the land where the dead lay,
   Kept by the care divine,
A bird in the heart of the red May,
   Sang to a spirit in mine,
Songs of a wonder olden,
   Seen by the eyes of youth,
In a nook of the volume golden,
   And a shrine of holy truth.
Thus when the fresh spring roses
   Break from their winter urns,
I stand like the prophet Moses,
   In front of a bush that burns.

Going to Bed.

NOW is it time for rest; 'tis the desire
   Of Sleep, our gentle comforter, and I
Have seen another pilgrim day expire;
   I wonder when 'twill be my turn to die,

And which of all the pilgrim days ahead
    Will leave me dead.

It is a thought which chants me fun'ral airs,
    While from my fading fire I turn away;
I hear it as I climb my chamber stairs,
    Saying stern words about a coming day,
That will to God go down in its death bed,
    Leaving me dead.

Then stranger forms will climb this path to take
    The measure of my corpse, a ghastly thing;
And when they lift me up I shall not wake
    Out of my sleep profound, nor when they bring
A coffin to my room I shall not dread,
    In sleep so dead.

Have I not trusted the Great God of life
    Ten thousand nights and more? Has he not sent
Sleep to refresh me from my daily strife,
    And morn to wake me when the night was spent;
Cannot I trust Him when by sickness led
    To my death bed?

Dead! what is death? All things are prone to change
    That are or will be; the great blazing sun,
This green-robed world, and these grand orbs that
      range
    The wilderness of space, all these shall run
Into the arms of death, nay, change instead
    Of being dead.

www.ingramcontent.com/pod-product-compliance
Lightning Source LLC
Chambersburg PA
CBHW030311170426
43202CB00009B/968